D1524389

TEEN RIGHTS AND FREEDOMS

| Search and Seizure

TEEN RIGHTS AND FREEDOMS

I Search and Seizure

Noël Merino
Book Editor

GREENHAVEN PRESS
A part of Gale, Cengage Learning

GALE
CENGAGE Learning·

Detroit • New York • San Francisco • New Haven, Conn • Waterville, Maine • London

Elizabeth Des Chenes, *Director, Publishing Solutions*

© 2013 Greenhaven Press, a part of Gale, Cengage Learning

Gale and Greenhaven Press are registered trademarks used herein under license.

For more information, contact:
Greenhaven Press
27500 Drake Rd.
Farmington Hills, MI 48331-3535
Or you can visit our Internet site at gale.cengage.com.

For product information and technology assistance, contact us at:

Gale Customer Support, 1-800-877-4253.
For permission to use material from this text or product, submit all requests online at www.cengage.com/permissions.

Further permissions questions can be emailed to permissionrequest@cengage.com.

Articles in Greenhaven Press anthologies are often edited for length to meet page requirements. In addition, original titles of these works are changed to clearly present the main thesis and to explicitly indicate the author's opinion. Every effort is made to ensure the Greenhaven Press accurately reflects the original intent of the authors. Every effort has been made to trace the owners of copyrighted material.

Cover Image © Brandon Bourdages/Shutterstock.com.

LIBRARY OF CONGRESS CATALOGING-IN-PUBLICATION DATA

Search and seizure / Noël Merino, book editor.
  p. cm. -- (Teen rights and freedoms)
  Includes bibliographical references and index.
  ISBN 978-0-7377-6403-1 (hardcover)
  1. Teenagers--Legal status, laws, etc.--United States. 2. Searches and seizures--United States. I. Merino, Noël, editor of compilation.
  KF479.S47 2013
  345.73'0722--dc23

                                                        2012036912

Printed in the United States of America
1 2 3 4 5 6 7 17 16 15 14 13

Contents

1. **The Interpretation of the Fourth Amendment Has Changed over Time**   10

   Russell L. Weaver

   A law professor contends that the meaning of the Fourth Amendment's protection against unreasonable searches and seizures continues to be refined by the US Supreme Court.

2. **Fourth Amendment Rights of Students Are Tempered by Security Concerns**   21

   David L. Hudson Jr.

   A legal scholar explains that students have a Fourth Amendment right to be free from unreasonable searches and seizures, but that right is limited by concerns for public school safety.

3. **Public Schools May Search Students in Order to Maintain Discipline**   30

   The Supreme Court's Decision

   Byron White

   The US Supreme Court rules that although students have a legitimate expectation of privacy, schools may search students if reasonable suspicion warrants it.

4. **Schools May Test Students Involved in Athletics for Drugs**   40

   The Supreme Court's Decision

   Antonin Scalia

The US Supreme Court rules that drug testing of student athletes serves an important government interest and does not violate the constitutional rights of students.

Virginia's attorney general argues that school officials may confiscate and search students' cellular phones and laptops when reasonable suspicion of breaking the law or school rules exists.

Foreword

"In the truest sense freedom cannot be bestowed, it must be achieved."
Franklin D. Roosevelt,
September 16, 1936

The notion of children and teens having rights is a relatively recent development. Early in American history, the head of the household—nearly always the father—exercised complete control over the children in the family. Children were legally considered to be the property of their parents. Over time, this view changed, as society began to acknowledge that children have rights independent of their parents, and that the law should protect young people from exploitation. By the early twentieth century, more and more social reformers focused on the welfare of children, and over the ensuing decades advocates worked to protect them from harm in the workplace, to secure public education for all, and to guarantee fair treatment for youths in the criminal justice system. Throughout the twentieth century, rights for children and teens—and restrictions on those rights—were established by Congress and reinforced by the courts. Today's courts are still defining and clarifying the rights and freedoms of young people, sometimes expanding those rights and sometimes limiting them. Some teen rights are outside the scope of public law and remain in the realm of the family, while still others are determined by school policies.

Each volume in the Teen Rights and Freedoms series focuses on a different right or freedom and offers an anthology of key essays and articles on that right or freedom and the responsibilities that come with it. Material within each volume is drawn from a diverse selection of primary and secondary sources—journals, magazines, newspapers, nonfiction books, organization newsletters, position papers, speeches, and government documents, with a particular emphasis on Supreme Court and lower court decisions. Volumes also include first-person narratives from young people and others involved in teen rights issues, such as parents and educators. The material is selected and arranged to highlight all the major social and legal controversies relating to the right or freedom under discussion. Each selection is preceded by an introduction that provides context and background. In many cases, the essays point to the difference between adult and teen rights, and why this difference exists.

Many of the volumes cover rights guaranteed under the Bill of Rights and how these rights are interpreted and protected in regard to children and teens, including freedom of speech, freedom of the press, due process, and religious rights. The scope of the series also encompasses rights or freedoms, whether real or perceived, relating to the school environment, such as electronic devices, dress, Internet policies, and privacy. Some volumes focus on the home environment, including topics such as parental control and sexuality.

Numerous features are included in each volume of Teen Rights and Freedoms:

- An annotated **table of contents** provides a brief summary of each essay in the volume and highlights court decisions and personal narratives.
- An **introduction** specific to the volume topic gives context for the right or freedom and its impact on daily life.
- A brief **chronology** offers important dates associated with the right or freedom, including landmark court cases.
- **Primary sources**—including personal narratives and court decisions—are among the varied selections in the anthology.
- **Illustrations**—including photographs, charts, graphs, tables, statistics, and maps—are closely tied to the text and chosen to help readers understand key points or concepts.

- An annotated list of **organizations to contact** presents sources of additional information on the topic.
- A **for further reading** section offers a bibliography of books, periodical articles, and Internet sources for further research.
- A comprehensive subject **index** provides access to key people, places, events, and subjects cited in the text.

Each volume of Teen Rights and Freedoms delves deeply into the issues most relevant to the lives of teens: their own rights, freedoms, and responsibilities. With the help of this series, students and other readers can explore from many angles the evolution and current expression of rights both historic and contemporary.

Introduction

The Fourth Amendment to the US Constitution delineates individual rights regarding searches and seizures. It reads:

> The right of the people to be secure in their persons, houses, papers, and effects, against unreasonable searches and seizures, shall not be violated, and no Warrants shall issue, but upon probable cause, supported by Oath or affirmation, and particularly describing the place to be searched, and the persons or things to be seized.

The Fourth Amendment guarantees individuals freedom from searches and seizures by government officials that are not justified by probable cause. The definition of probable cause—and hence the conditions under which individuals may be searched, with or without a warrant—has been defined and refined over the years by the US Supreme Court.

The court has delineated areas of reasonable searches limited by expectations of privacy. The Fourth Amendment protects the right to privacy in situations where privacy is to be expected. Thus, although there is little expectation of privacy in public or in one's car, there is an expectation of privacy in one's home and in pertaining to one's body. In general, the court has determined that before individuals or their property are searched by law enforcement, a warrant must be obtained from a judge. However, there are numerous exceptions to the warrant requirement, especially in places where there is little expectation of privacy, including when an individual consents to a search, when the search is solely to look for weapons, when the search is deemed immediately necessary for public safety, when the search is at the border, or when the search is of an automobile. For minors, the court has determined that school officials may conduct searches in order to maintain safety and discipline in the school setting.

In 1985, the US Supreme Court ruled in *New Jersey v. T.L.O.* that although students have some reasonable expectation of privacy at school, public school officials may search students if it is necessary to maintain discipline. Similarly, in *Vernonia School District v. Acton* (1995), the court ruled that schools may maintain discipline by requiring drug tests for athletes. The court extended its reasoning from the *Vernonia* decision in *Board of Education v. Earls* (2002), allowing schools to drug test all students involved in extracurricular activities. Most recently, the court in *Safford Unified School District #1 v. Redding* (2009) ruled in favor of student privacy rights, finding that a strip search of a student warrants greater justification than would be required when merely searching belongings.

The above US Supreme Court decisions illustrate how the Fourth Amendment right to freedom from unreasonable searches and seizures is limited for teenagers within the school setting. At the core of the difference between the Fourth Amendment right of teenagers and that of adults is the fact that minors are under the care of parents and teachers. Because of this, parents and those acting in the place of parents may take actions that impinge on minors' expectation of privacy in order to meet their caretaking duties. In public schools, a teenager's right to freedom from unreasonable searches and seizures is tempered by the need of school officials to maintain order and discipline.

The Fourth Amendment protection against unreasonable searches and seizures limits the ability of government officials to defy expectations of privacy. Nonetheless, this protection is not without exceptions, and the court has delineated many realms where searches and seizures are allowed. *Teen Rights and Freedoms: Search and Seizure* explores a variety of court decisions regarding the Fourth Amendment and their impact on the privacy rights of students.

Chronology

1914　　　　In *Weeks v. United States* the US Supreme Court sets forth the exclusionary rule, which prohibits the admission in the federal court system of evidence obtained by warrantless seizure in violation of the Fourth Amendment.

1961　　　　In *Mapp v. Ohio* the US Supreme Court holds that the exclusionary rule applies to the states as well as the federal government.

1967　　　　In *Katz v. United States* the US Supreme Court extends Fourth Amendment protection from unreasonable searches and seizures to areas where people have a reasonable expectation of privacy, such as phone conversations.

1968　　　　In *Terry v. Ohio* the US Supreme Court holds that it is not a violation of the Fourth Amendment for police to frisk a suspect who is reasonably believed to be involved in criminal activity.

1979　　　　In *Delaware v. Prouse* the US Supreme Court holds that police may not pull a motorist over simply to check license and registration, but must have reasonable suspicion of criminal activity.

In *Dunaway v. New York* the US Supreme Court holds that police may not detain a suspect without probable cause.

1980

In *Payton v. New York* the US Supreme Court rules that the police or government agents cannot enter a home to arrest its occupant without a warrant or consent of the occupant.

1983

In *United States v. Knotts* the US Supreme Court holds that the use of electronic surveillance devices tracking movement on public streets is not a violation of the Fourth Amendment.

In *United States v. Place* the US Supreme Court finds that a temporary seizure of personal property in order to gain a warrant is permissible only if such investigative detention is limited.

1984

In *United States v. Karo* the US Supreme Court determines that use of electronic surveillance devices tracking movement within the home is a violation of the Fourth Amendment.

1985

In *New Jersey v. T.L.O.* the US Supreme Court decides that although students have a legitimate expectation of privacy, schools may search students if reasonable suspicion warrants it.

1989   In *Florida v. Riley* the US Supreme Court holds that a homeowner has no expectation of privacy from a police flyby over one's property.

1990   In *Michigan Department of State Police v. Sitz* the US Supreme Court determines that it is not a violation of the Fourth Amendment for police to set up sobriety checkpoints and stop drivers to examine them for intoxication.

1991   In *California v. Acevedo* the US Supreme Court decides that law enforcement may search an entire vehicle, including closed containers, if the police have probable cause.

1995   In *Vernonia School District 47J v. Acton* the US Supreme Court rules that drug testing of student athletes does not violate the constitutional rights of young people under the Fourth Amendment.

1998   In *Knowles v. Iowa* the US Supreme Court determines that the Fourth Amendment prohibits law enforcement from searching a vehicle after stopping the vehicle for a moving violation citation.

2000   In *City of Indianapolis v. Edmond* the US Supreme Court holds that it is a violation of the Fourth Amendment for law enforcement to conduct drug searches at roadblocks.

2001   In *Kyllo v. United States* the US Supreme Court holds that the use of thermal imaging to search a home requires a warrant under the Fourth Amendment.

2002   In *Board of Education v. Earls* the US Supreme Court rules that a school policy of testing students involved in extracurricular activities for drugs is not a significant invasion of student's privacy.

2009   In *Safford Unified School District #1 v. Redding* the US Supreme Court rules that although schools may search students when there is a reasonable suspicion of danger, searches without justification are unconstitutional.

2012   In *United States v. Jones* the US Supreme Court rules that warrantless use of a tracking device on a motor vehicle by law enforcement is an unconstitutional search under the Fourth Amendment.

> *"While the Fourth Amendment retains a central place in American jurisprudence, the US Supreme Court's interpretation of the Fourth Amendment has changed over time."*

The Interpretation of the Fourth Amendment Has Changed over Time

Russell L. Weaver

In the following viewpoint, a law professor argues that although the Fourth Amendment was originally drafted to prevent the unlawful search of people in their homes, the protection against unreasonable searches and seizures has expanded over the years to encompass a right to privacy of the person. The author contends that although a preference for obtaining warrants to conduct a search under the Fourth Amendment has been established, many exceptions are allowed under the law for warrantless searches and seizures. Russell L. Weaver is a law professor at the University of Louisville's Louis D. Brandeis School of Law.

Although the U.S. Constitution was originally drafted without a Bill of Rights, the people demanded protection against various forms of governmental intrusion as a condition of ratifica-

Russell L. Weaver, "Search and Seizure," *Encyclopedia of the Supreme Court of the United States*, 1st ed., vol. 4. New York: Macmillan Reference USA, 2009, pp. 347–352. Copyright © 2009 by Cengage Learning. All rights reserved. Reproduced by permission.

tion. One of the protections they required was against unreasonable searches and seizures. During the colonial period the British troops used writs of assistance and so-called general warrants, which permitted broad searches of colonists' homes and person, essentially allowing British troops to search colonists' dwellings and persons whenever and wherever they wanted, including broad searches encompassing entire homes. Hostility to the writs of assistance and general warrants was the "driving force" behind the demand for protections, as was "widespread hostility among the former Colonists to the issuance of writs of assistance" [*United States v. Verdugo-Urquidez* (1990)]. Indeed, as the Court recognized in *Boyd v. United States* (1886) that the "writs of assistance . . . were fresh in the memories of those who achieved our independence and established our form of government."

The Protection of People, Not Places

While the Fourth Amendment retains a central place in American jurisprudence, the U.S. Supreme Court's interpretation of the Fourth Amendment has changed over time. During the colonial period, the focus was on searches of the individual's house, papers, or effects. In other words, a search occurred when government intruded into a "constitutionally protected area" [*Katz v. United States* (1967)]. As a result, a search would occur when the police intruded into someone's house or on the curtilage surrounding the house. Absent a trespass or an intrusion, the Fourth Amendment was not violated.

However, in the *Katz* case the Court moved away from the notion of constitutionally protected areas and held that the Fourth Amendment protects people rather than just places. As a result, the focus shifted away from whether there was a trespass into a constitutionally protected area to whether there was a violation of an individual's expectation of privacy: "There is a twofold requirement, first that a person have exhibited an actual (subjective) expectation of privacy and, second, that the expectation be one that society is prepared to recognize as 'reasonable.'" As a result, those things that "a person knowingly exposes to the public, even in his own home or office, is not a subject of Fourth Amendment protection. But what he seeks to preserve as private, even in an area accessible to the public, may be constitutionally protected."

The importance of the *Katz* test was evident in the holding in that case. *Katz* involved an effort by police to record the contents of a conversation made from a public telephone. Under the Court's prior precedent, there could be no search within the meaning of the Fourth Amendment because there was no intrusion into a constitutionally protected area. In *Katz,* the Court found a search despite the absence of such an intrusion:

> One who occupies [a public phone booth], shuts the door behind him, and pays the toll that permits him to place a call is surely entitled to assume that the words he utters into the mouthpiece will not be broadcast to the world. To read the Constitution more narrowly is to ignore the vital role that the public telephone has come to play in private communication.

Katz's "reasonable expectation of privacy" test has grown in importance as technology has evolved and improved. When the nation was founded, the police (and other governmental officials) had limited forms of technology at their disposal to spy on individuals. Over the centuries, the nature of technology has changed to the point that technology threatens to undermine and overwhelm an individual's right to privacy. Indeed, in the early twenty-first century, merchants advertise listening devices that will allow an individual to overhear what people who are far away (in the sense of being beyond normal hearing distance) are saying. In *Katz,* the police used a recording device to listen to the content of Katz's conversation from a distance.

The Fourth Amendment and New Technologies

The Court's handling of these new technologies has varied. For example, in *United States v. Knotts* (1983), the police placed a tracking beeper inside a container that was delivered to a suspect, and then used the beeper's signals to follow the defendant's car to a remote cabin where he was operating a drug laboratory. Even though the police did not maintain visual surveillance of the vehicle, the beeper allowed them to be aware of its whereabouts. The Court sustained the police actions, noting that a "person traveling in an automobile on public thoroughfares has no reasonable expectation of privacy in his movements from one place to another . . . [Nothing] in the Fourth Amendment prohibited the police from augmenting [their] sensory facilities with such enhancement as science and technology afforded them [here]."

In the Court's subsequent decision in *United States v. Karo* (1984), the Court invalidated the use of a beeper used to determine information regarding the interior of a suspect's property and the movement of items within that property. The *Karo* Court found that a violation of a reasonable expectation of privacy did occur when police in *Karo* used a beeper in a container to discover "a critical fact about the interior of the premises" that the government "would not have otherwise obtained without a warrant."

A number of cases have also involved surveillance from airplanes. In general, the Court has upheld these searches. For example, in *Florida v. Riley* (1989), the Court held that a homeowner has no reasonable expectation of privacy against a police flyby over his or her property even though the police fly quite low (400 feet). Likewise, in *Dow Chemical v. United States* (1986), the Court sustained the use of an aerial mapping camera during a fly over commercial property. Both *Riley* and *Dow Chemical* reasoned that members of the "flying public" could make "naked eye" observations of the curtilage, and could use a "conventional" mapping camera such as the one in *Dow Chemical.*

In the *Dow Chemical* case, the Court predicted that someday it would be confronted by police use of "an electronic device [to] penetrate walls or windows." That issue was presented in *Kyllo v. United States* (2001), a case involving a "thermal imaging device" that allowed the police to track the level of heat emanating from a house. In *Kyllo*, the police stood across the street from a private home and aimed the device at the house. The results of the scan suggested that the garage was hotter than the rest of the house and "substantially warmer than neighboring homes." The police used this evidence to help establish the probable cause necessary to procure a warrant to search the home. During the warrant search, they discovered that the occupant was growing marijuana in the house using halide lights (which were what produced the heat). *Kyllo* held that the homeowner possessed a reasonable expectation of privacy against police use of the thermal imaging device, and rendered a broad home-protective ruling:

> We think that obtaining by sense-enhancing technology any information regarding the interior of the home that could not otherwise have been obtained without physical 'intrusion into a constitutionally protected area' constitutes a search—at least where (as here) the technology in question is not in general public use. This assures preservation of that degree of privacy against government that existed when the Fourth Amendment was adopted.

The *Kyllo* majority rejected the government's argument that the heat device detected heat only from the external surface of the home, reasoning that such a "mechanical interpretation" of privacy was rejected in *Katz*. The *Kyllo* majority was also very protective of distinctive privacy protections accorded the home. The Court noted that [*United States*] *v. Karo [1984]* suggests that a homeowner should not be subject to police use of technology that may discern human activity inside the home. Moreover, the Court rejected the government's argument that the heat device did not "detect private activities occurring in private areas," reasoning that "in the home, all details are intimate details, because the entire area is held safe from prying government eyes." *Kyllo* may reflect the Court's concern, and the Court's attempt, to protect homes (and, more to the point, homeowners) against the steady advance of technology.

A thermogram—which detects temperature variations in a building—shows a person waving inside a home. The US Supreme Court has ruled that using thermal imaging on suspects' homes is illegal without a warrant. © Photo Researchers.

The Warrant Preference

The U.S. Supreme Court has repeatedly emphasized that, whereas the Fourth Amendment does not require a warrant for all searches, it does suggest a "'strong preference for searches conducted pursuant to a warrant'" [*Ornelas v. United States* (1996), quoting *Illinois v. Gates* (1983)]. In other words, "'searches conducted outside the judicial process, without prior approval by judge or magistrate, are *per se* unreasonable under the Fourth Amendment—subject only to a few specifically established and well delineated exceptions'" [*Thompson v. Louisiana* (1984), quoting *Katz*]. However, as shall be seen, there are numerous exceptions to the warrant requirement, and numerous situations when the courts sustain both warrantless searches and warrantless seizures notwithstanding the warrant preference.

Neutral and Detached Magistrates. There are several reasons for the warrant preference. First, before a warrant can issue, the police must submit their evidence to "the detached scrutiny of a neutral magistrate" [*United States v. Leon* (1984)]. As a result, rather than leave the protection of an individual's home, papers, and effects to "the hurried judgment of a law enforcement officer 'engaged in the often competitive enterprise of ferreting out crime,'" the determination of whether a search would be allowed was to be resolved by a neutral judicial official [*Leon*, quoting *United States v. Chadwick* (1977), quoting *Johnson v. United States* (1948) and *United States v. Ventresca* (1965)]. The magistrate thus serves as a bulwark between the citizenry and the police. Second, a "warrant assures the citizen that the intrusion is authorized by law, and that it is narrowly limited in its objectives and scope" [*Skinner v. Railway Labor Executives' Association* (1989)].

Probable Cause Requirement. Before a warrant can issue, the magistrate must find that probable cause exists. In other words, a warrant may not issue based on a suspicion or a hunch, but must be grounded in an objective finding of probable cause. Obviously, the police would be more effective in ferreting out crime if they could search anyone, at any time, without any justification. However, in order to protect individual privacy, and create a system consistent with individual freedom in a free society, the Constitution provides the probable cause requirement as an additional buffer between the citizenry and the police. For an arrest, this means that there must be probable cause to believe that a crime has been committed, and that the person to be arrested committed it. For a search, the Fourth Amendment demands a showing of probable cause that the fruits, instrumentalities, or evidence of crime can be found at the place to be searched.

Particularity Requirement. An additional requirement of the Fourth Amendment is that the warrant must particularly de-

The Fourth Amendment to the US Constitution

The right of the people to be secure in their persons, houses, papers, and effects, against unreasonable searches and seizures, shall not be violated, and no warrants shall issue, but upon probable cause, supported by oath or affirmation, and particularly describing the place to be searched, and the persons or things to be seized.

scribe both the place to be searched, and the persons or things to be seized. The particularity requirement was inserted in the Fourth Amendment in response to the general warrants issued during the colonial period. General warrants and writs of assistance essentially allowed British troops to rummage through a colonist's entire home (as well as the colonist's papers and effects). The objective of the requirement was to limit the search "to the specific areas and things for which there is probable cause to search," and thereby to ensure "that the search will be carefully tailored to its justifications, and will not take on the character of the wide-ranging exploratory searches the Framers intended to prohibit" [*Maryland v. Garrison* (1987)].

Warrantless Searches and Seizures

Although the Fourth Amendment prohibits "unreasonable searches and seizures," it does not explicitly require that either searches or seizures be conducted pursuant to a warrant. The Court has articulated a preference for warrants, but it has frequently found that warrantless searches are reasonable. Moreover, the Court distinguishes between warrantless arrests and warrantless searches. Even though warrantless arrests are generally permissible, warrantless searches are disfavored and are "per se unreasonable subject only to a few specifically established and well-delineated exceptions" (*Katz*).

The exceptions to the warrant requirement are many and varied. The exceptions involve the following:

- plain view exception
- search incident to legal arrest exception, which allows the police to search the area within an arrestee's immediate control following a valid arrest
- booking exception, which allows jail authorities to search someone who is about to be incarcerated in a jail population
- automobile exception, which allows the police to search an automobile without a warrant provided that they have probable cause for the search
- inventory exception, which allows the police to inventory the contents of a vehicle that has been lawfully impounded
- consent exception, which allows the police to search a person or place provided that consent is given
- administrative exception, which applies special rules to inspections by administrative officials
- exigent circumstances exception, which allows the police to make warrantless searches in certain emergency contexts
- exception for searches conducted at or near the border to prevent illegal aliens or contraband from being smuggled into the country.

Stop and Frisk Exception. Perhaps the greatest area of growth for warrantless searches has come in the stop and frisk arena. Following the U.S. Supreme Court's landmark decision in *Terry v. Ohio* (1968), the Court has created a variety of rules governing police-citizen encounters. In these cases, the Court has articulated new exceptions to the warrant requirement by balancing the degree of intrusion on the individual against the public interest or need for the intrusion. Using this test, in *Terry*, the Court held that when the police reasonably suspect that individuals are involved in criminal activity, and that they are armed and dangerous, the police may stop and "frisk" the suspects. In other words, the police might subject them to a "pat down" for weapons. Whereas an arrest would still require probable cause, police could take the lesser actions involved with a stop and frisk based on less evidence of wrongdoing—a reasonable suspicion.

Investigative Stops of Automobiles (and Other Seizures). Courts have used the *Terry* balancing test to create a series of rules governing police-citizen encounters. For example, the Court has held that police may not make an "investigative stop" of an individual without a reasonable suspicion that the individual is involved in criminal activity. For example, in *Delaware v. Prouse* (1979), the Court held that the police may not pull a motorist over simply to check a driver's license and registration. In order to justify a traffic stop, the police must have a reasonable suspicion that the individual is involved in criminal activity. Likewise, in *Dunaway v. New York* (1979), the Court held that the police may not pick up and transport a suspect to the station for questioning absent probable cause. In *Davis v. Mississippi* (1969), the Court held that probable cause is also required when the police want to pick up and transport a suspect to the station for fingerprinting. . . .

Special Needs Searches. Terry's need-intrusion test has also been used to create a series of other so-called special needs exceptions to the warrant requirement. For example, in *Skinner*, the Court upheld Federal Railroad Administration (FRA) regulations mandating blood and urine tests of railroad employees involved in "major" train accidents, and authorizing railroads to administer breath and urine tests to employees who violate certain safety rules. Warrants were not required.

Likewise, in *Vernonia School District v. Acton* (1995), the Court upheld a school policy providing for the suspicionless drug testing of school athletes. While the Court agreed that the testing implicated Fourth Amendment interests (the collection and analysis of drug samples involved a search), the Court concluded that a warrant and probable cause might be inappropriate in this context because such requirements "would unduly interfere with the maintenance of the swift and informal disciplinary procedures [that are] needed."

In *Board of Education of Independent School District v. Earls* (2002), the Court upheld drug tests for all students involved in extracurricular activities. The Court noted that "special needs" are involved in the public school context, and that "Fourth Amendment rights . . . are different in public schools" because schools have custodial and tutelary responsibility for children. . . .

When the police (or other governmental officials) violate the Fourth Amendment, the citizen might seek any of a variety of remedies. A remedy that is frequently sought is exclusion of any evidence (obtained during an illegal search) from a subsequent criminal trial. While there are limits on the so-called exclusionary rule, it remains a potent weapon for deterring police misconduct. However, other remedies are available, including the possibility of civil suits under state or local laws, or under the U.S. Constitution or various civil rights statutes.

| "Fourth Amendment issues in public
  schools arise with frequency."

Fourth Amendment Rights of Students Are Tempered by Security Concerns

David L. Hudson Jr.

In the following viewpoint, a scholar argues that although students in public schools do have Fourth Amendment rights, because of the need for school officials to maintain a safe learning environment, those rights are often constrained. The author claims that several court decisions have upheld the constitutionality of searches of students' belongings, allowing school officials more leeway than law enforcement officials outside of the school setting. However, he notes that strip searches have been found to be unconstitutional in most situations. In addition, the author maintains that despite challenges under the Fourth Amendment, drug testing of students has been found to be an acceptable practice in the public school setting. David L. Hudson Jr. is a scholar at the First Amendment Center at Vanderbilt University.

David L. Hudson Jr., "The Fourth Amendment in Public Schools: Many Important Fourth Amendment Cases Involve Students," *Insights on Law & Society*, vol. 11, no. 2, May 2011, pp. 14–15, 26, 29. Copyright © 2011 by American Bar Association. All rights reserved. Reproduced by permission.

Locker searches, car searches, pat-down searches, confiscation of cell phones, random drug tests, the use of metal detectors, and the list continues. School officials regularly conduct searches and seizures of students ostensibly to fulfill their paramount duty of providing a safe learning environment. In a post-Columbine environment, safety concerns often trump other considerations. Students often counter that these searches and seizures infringe on their privacy interests and violate their constitutional rights. They argue that they are persons under the Constitution, deserving of respect and dignity. The question becomes whether the actions of school officials furthers a reasonable way of protecting students from danger or whether it crosses a constitutional line and violates the Fourth Amendment of the U.S. Constitution.

The Fourth Amendment

The Fourth Amendment provides individuals with privacy and protection from invasive conduct by government officials. It normally requires law enforcement officials to have a warrant backed up by probable cause before they can search a person's belongings or seize the person. The lynchpin of Fourth Amendment law is individualized suspicion that a particular person is harboring contraband or poses a threat to society.

The text of the Fourth Amendment reads: "The right of the people to be secure in their persons, houses, papers, and effects, against unreasonable searches and seizures, shall not be violated, and no Warrants shall issue, but upon probable cause, supported by Oath or affirmation, and particularly describing the place to be searched, and the persons or things to be seized."

Several key points of Fourth Amendment jurisprudence are: (1) The Fourth Amendment does not prohibit all searches and seizures, only those that are "unreasonable;" (2) A search conducted pursuant to a warrant backed up by probable cause is reasonable; and (3) Roving searches generally are prohibited, and searches are supposed to be particular—searching a particular person for particular items.

If a search or seizure is deemed to violate an individual's Fourth Amendment rights, evidence from that search must be suppressed or not brought into evidence under the exclusionary rule. This rule provides, that, if the police violate the Fourth Amendment, the evidence becomes a "fruit of the poisonous tree" and must be excluded.

The Constitutionality of School Searches

The U.S. Supreme Court addressed the constitutionality of school searches in its 1985 decision *New Jersey v. T.L.O.* The case arose out of a March 1980 incident at Piscataway High School. A teacher discovered two girls in the lavatory smoking. The teacher sent them to vice principal Theodore Choplick, who interrogated the two girls. One girl admitted to smoking but a girl identified in court papers by her initials "T.L.O." denied the charge.

Choplick then searched her purse, finding a pack of cigarettes and a pack of rolling papers. He knew that rolling papers were associated with marijuana so he continued to search her purse, finding a pipe, a small amount of marijuana, plastic bags and index cards with initials beside small amounts of money. He suspected T.L.O. of selling marijuana and contacted the girl's mother and the police. The state pursued delinquency charges against T.L.O.

In juvenile court, T.L.O.'s attorney argued that the evidence of marijuana should be suppressed because Choplick violated her Fourth Amendment rights and engaged in an unreasonable search. The state countered that the Fourth Amendment did not apply in public schools and that Choplick was justified. The juvenile court ruled that the Fourth Amendment applied, but that Choplick had reasonable suspicion to conduct the search in question.

T.L.O. appealed and an intermediate appellate court affirmed the Fourth Amendment ruling. On farther appeal, the New Jersey Supreme Court reversed and found that Choplick violated

Key US Supreme Court Cases Involving the Fourth Amendment in Public Schools

School Searches: New Jersey v. T.L.O. (1985, Piscataway, NJ)

Student Athlete Drug Testing: Vernonia School District v. Acton (1995, Vernonia OR)

Drug Testing of Students in Extracurricular Activities: Board of Education v. Earls (2002, Tecumseh, OK)

Student Strip Searches: Safford Unified School District #1 v. Redding (2009, Safford, AZ)

T.L.O.'s Fourth Amendment rights by continuing to search her purse after finding cigarettes.

The state appealed to the U.S. Supreme Court, and argued that the Fourth Amendment applied to govern public school searches but that Choplick's search was reasonable. The state of New Jersey argued that school officials were acting *"in loco parentis"*—or were simply parents of the students. Just as parents are not subject to the Bill of Rights, the state reasoned, neither are school officials.

The Court's Decision

The Court rejected that far-reaching argument, noting that public school officials act not from parents' permission but from state-imposed duties and rules. "In carrying out searches and other disciplinary functions pursuant to such policies, school officials act as representatives of the State, not merely as surrogates for the parents, and they cannot claim the parents' immunity from the strictures of the Fourth Amendment," Justice Byron White wrote in his majority opinion.

However, the Court also rejected T.L.O's argument that the traditional requirements of a warrant and probable cause were required. The majority reasoned that the warrant requirement was too impractical for the public school environment: "The warrant requirement, in particular, is unsuited to the school environment: requiring a teacher to obtain a warrant before searching a child suspected of an infraction of school rules (or of the criminal law) would unduly interfere with the maintenance of the swift and informal disciplinary procedures needed in the schools."

The Court also relaxed the level of suspicion in the school environment, writing: "The school setting also requires some modification of the level of suspicion of illicit activity needed to justify a search." The Court determined that probable cause also was too rigid a requirement and that school searches must simply meet a standard of reasonableness.

The Court determined that school searches of students are constitutional as long as they are (1) justified at inception, and (2) reasonably related in scope to the circumstances that justified the search in the first place.

Justice White and the majority determined that Choplick's search of T.L.O's purse was reasonable. . . . He had reason to believe that T.L.O. had been smoking in the lavatory and the discovery of rolling papers justified a more thorough search of the purse's contents.

In his dissenting opinion, Justice William Brennan disagreed with the Court's discarding of the probable-cause standard: "I emphatically disagree with the Court's decision to cast aside the constitutional probable-cause standard when assessing the constitutional validity of a schoolhouse search."

In *State v. Taylor* (2010), a Louisiana appeals court applied the *T.L.O.* standard to find that a search of a student suspected of smoking in the bathroom violated the Fourth Amendment. In this case, a school official caught student Demond Taylor and other students smoking in the bathroom. Then, the official searched Taylor's shoes and found illegal drugs. A divided Louisiana appeals court upheld a trial court's ruling that the search of Taylor's shoes violated the Fourth Amendment, because it was not reasonable to expect that Taylor might have cigarettes in his shoes. The dissent ruled that it was not very intrusive to require Taylor to remove his shoes.

Strip Searches of Students

Strip searches are more invasive than other types of searches. The U.S. Supreme Court ruled in *Safford Unified School District v. Redding* (2009) that school officials violated the Fourth Amendment rights of middle school student Savana Redding when they subjected her to a strip search because they thought she might be carrying prescription drugs.

School officials, including assistant principal Kerry Wilson, had heard that some students had prescription pills at school. A school official had confiscated four pills of Ibuprofen and a [day] planner. When queried by Wilson, the student said that the pills and the planner were Savana Redding's.

Wilson then went to Redding's math class and removed her from the class. Wilson searched Redding's purse but found no contraband. He then ordered a school nurse to conduct a personal search of Redding, who had to pull out the elastic of her underwear and expose her breast and pelvic areas. The search revealed no pills or other contraband.

The school officials tried to use the *T.L.O.* precedent as support for the search of Redding. But the Supreme Court determined that the strip search was excessive because the pills were not dangerous and there was no reason to think that Redding might be carrying contraband in her underwear. The Court made "clear that the *T.L.O.* concern to limit a school search to reasonable scope requires the support of reasonable suspicion of danger or of resort to underwear for hiding evidence of wrong-

Locker searches with drug-sniffing dogs are among the many methods schools use to investigate students' property. ©John Suchocki/The Republican/Landov.

doing before a search can reasonably make the quantum leap from outer clothes and backpacks to exposure of intimate parts."

The majority concluded: "In sum, what was missing from the suspected facts that pointed to Savana was any indication of danger to the students from the power of the drugs or their quantity, and any reason to suppose that Savana was carrying pills in her underwear. We think that the combination of these deficiencies was fatal to finding the search reasonable."

Drug Testing of Students

The U.S. Supreme Court has ruled that public school officials can conduct random drug tests of student athletes and all students who participate in extracurricular activities in *Vernonia School District v. Acton* (1995) and *Board of Education v. Earls* (2002).

The Vernonia School District in Oregon required athletes to submit to random drug tests after witnessing an alleged rise in student drug use in the 1980s. Some athletes supposedly were the leaders of the so-called drug culture. District officials initially tried counseling and various antidrug messages, but those did not work sufficiently. The district then initiated a drug-testing program.

James Acton, an incoming seventh-grader, and his parents objected to the drug-testing as an invasion of privacy. They challenged the constitutionality of the program in federal court. A federal district court rejected the lawsuit, but the 9th U.S. Circuit Court of Appeals ruled that the policy violated the Fourth Amendment and a corresponding provision of the Oregon Constitution.

On appeal, the U.S. Supreme Court reversed, ruling 6-3 that the policy was constitutional and reasonable. School officials did not need individualized suspicion before drug testing athletes and that the drug use in the public schools created a "special needs" exception to such testing. The majority also noted that athletes have reduced privacy expectations in the public schools. "Legitimate privacy expectations are even less with regard to student athletes," Justice Antonin Scalia wrote in his majority opinion.

The majority cited three factors in support of the drug-testing policy: (1) the decreased privacy expectations; (2) the "relative unobtrusiveness" of the search and seizure; and (3) the severe need for the policy at the school.

Several years later, the Court upheld a drug-testing policy in Tecumseh, Oklahoma, that required all middle and high school students who wished to participate in extracurricular activities to submit to random drug testing. Students Lindsay Earls, a prospective band member, and Daniel James, a prospective member of the Academic Team, challenged the policy.

The Court upheld the policy by a narrow 5-4 ruling in *Board of Education v. Earls* (2002), extending the rationale of the *Acton* case from athletes to all students participating in extracurricular activities. "Schoolchildren are routinely required to submit to physical examinations and vaccinations against disease," the Court noted.

Four justices dissented, including Justice Ruth Bader Ginsburg, who had voted to uphold the drug-testing policy in the *Acton* case. "The particular testing program upheld today is not reasonable, it is capricious, even perverse."

Even though the U.S. Supreme Court twice has upheld drug-testing programs, students and their parents have challenged these programs under respective state constitutions with mixed results. For example, the Washington Supreme Court invalidated a student athlete drug-testing policy in *York v. Wahkiakum School District* (2008), while the Indiana Supreme Court upheld a drug-testing policy in *Northwestern School Corp. v. Linke* (2002).

Fourth Amendment issues in public schools arise with frequency. Generally, officials comport with the Constitution when they search students based upon individualized suspicion that the student harbors contraband, carries a weapon, or otherwise violates school rules. Highly publicized school shootings dramatize the need for school officials to take safety issues seriously. At the same time, mass searches of students—outside of a general metal detector or drug-testing policies—may be viewed as excessively intrusive. The Court's recent decision in the Savana Redding case serves as a reminder of the delicate balance between students' constitutional rights and public school security.

> "The legality of a search of a student should depend simply on the reasonableness, under all the circumstances, of the search."

Public Schools May Search Students in Order to Maintain Discipline

The Supreme Court's Decision

Byron White

In the following viewpoint, a US Supreme Court justice contends that although students have Fourth Amendment rights, school officials may search students when it is deemed reasonable. The author argues that students' expectations of privacy need to be balanced with the needs of school officials to maintain order. He concludes that unlike outside of school, where the Fourth Amendment guarantees a search warrant or probable cause to justify a search, within school the correct standard is simply one of reasonableness in maintaining order. Byron White served as associate justice on the US Supreme Court from 1962 to 1993.

Byron White, Majority opinion, *New Jersey v. T.L.O.*, United States Supreme Court, January 15, 1985.

On March 7, 1980, a teacher at Piscataway High School in Middlesex County, N.J. discovered two girls smoking in a lavatory. One of the two girls was the respondent T.L.O, who at that time was a 14-year-old high school freshman. Because smoking in the lavatory was a violation of a school rule, the teacher took the two girls to the Principal's office, where they met with Assistant Vice Principal Theodore Choplick. In response to questioning by Mr. Choplick, T.L.O's companion admitted that she had violated the rule. T.L.O, however, denied that she had been smoking in the lavatory and claimed that she did not smoke at all.

Mr. Choplick asked T.L.O to come into his private office and demanded to see her purse. Opening the purse, he found a pack of cigarettes, which he removed from the purse and held before T.L.O as he accused her of having lied to him. As he reached into the purse for the cigarettes, Mr. Choplick also noticed a package of cigarette rolling papers. In his experience, possession of rolling papers by high school students was closely associated with the use of marihuana. Suspecting that a closer examination of the purse might yield further evidence of drug use, Mr. Choplick proceeded to search the purse thoroughly. The search revealed a small amount of marihuana, a pipe, a number of empty plastic bags, a substantial quantity of money in one-dollar bills, an index card that appeared to be a list of students who owed T.L.O money, and two letters that implicated T.L.O in marihuana dealing.

Mr. Choplick notified T.L.O's mother and the police, and turned the evidence of drug dealing over to the police. At the request of the police, T.L.O's mother took her daughter to police headquarters, where T.L.O confessed that she had been selling marihuana at the high school. On the basis of the confession and the evidence seized by Mr. Choplick, the State brought delinquency charges against T.L.O in the Juvenile and Domestic Relations Court of Middlesex County. Contending that Mr. Choplick's search of her purse violated the Fourth Amendment, T.L.O moved to suppress the evidence found in her purse as well as her confession, which, she argued, was tainted by the allegedly unlawful search. . . .

The Fourth Amendment in Public Schools

In determining whether the search at issue in this case violated the Fourth Amendment, we are faced initially with the question whether that Amendment's prohibition on unreasonable searches and seizures applies to searches conducted by public school officials. We hold that it does.

It is now beyond dispute that

> the Federal Constitution, by virtue of the Fourteenth Amendment, prohibits unreasonable searches and seizures by state officers [*Elkins v. United States* (1960)].

Equally indisputable is the proposition that the Fourteenth Amendment protects the rights of students against encroachment by public school officials:

> The Fourteenth Amendment, as now applied to the States, protects the citizen against the State itself and all of its creatures—Boards of Education not excepted. These have, of course, important, delicate, and highly discretionary functions, but none that they may not perform within the limits of the Bill of Rights. That they are educating the young for citizenship is reason for scrupulous protection of Constitutional freedoms of the individual, if we are not to strangle the free mind at its source and teach youth to discount important principles of our government as mere platitudes [*West Virginia State Bd. of Ed. v. Barnette* (1943)]. . . .

Notwithstanding the general applicability of the Fourth Amendment to the activities of civil authorities, a few courts have concluded that school officials are exempt from the dictates of the Fourth Amendment by virtue of the special nature of their authority over schoolchildren. Teachers and school administrators, it is said, act *in loco parentis* [in the place of a parent] in their dealings with students: their authority is that of the parent, not the State, and is therefore not subject to the limits of the Fourth Amendment.

Such reasoning is in tension with contemporary reality and the teachings of this Court. We have held school officials subject to the commands of the First Amendment and the Due Process Clause of the Fourteenth Amendment. If school authorities are state actors for purposes of the constitutional guarantees of freedom of expression and due process, it is difficult to understand why they should be deemed to be exercising parental rather than public authority when conducting searches of their students. More generally, the Court has recognized that "the concept of parental delegation" as a source of school authority is not entirely "consonant with compulsory education laws" [*Ingraham v. Wright* (1977)]. Today's public school officials do not merely exercise authority voluntarily conferred on them by individual parents; rather, they act in furtherance of publicly mandated educational and disciplinary policies. . . . In carrying out searches and other disciplinary functions pursuant to such policies, school officials act as representatives of the State, not merely as surrogates for the parents, and they cannot claim the parents' immunity from the strictures of the Fourth Amendment.

Balancing Privacy and Discipline

To hold that the Fourth Amendment applies to searches conducted by school authorities is only to begin the inquiry into the standards governing such searches. Although the underlying command of the Fourth Amendment is always that searches and seizures be reasonable, what is reasonable depends on the context within which a search takes place. The determination of the standard of reasonableness governing any specific class of searches requires "balancing the need to search against the invasion which the search entails" [*Camara v. Municipal Court* (1967)]. On one side of the balance are arrayed the individual's legitimate expectations of privacy and personal security; on the

In 1985 the US Supreme Court ruled that school officials are exempt from certain constitutional privacy protections and may search students' purses. © Laurence Mouton/PhotoAlto/Corbis.

other, the government's need for effective methods to deal with breaches of public order. . . .

Although this Court may take notice of the difficulty of maintaining discipline in the public schools today, the situation is not so dire that students in the schools may claim no legitimate expectations of privacy. We have recently recognized that the need to maintain order in a prison is such that prisoners retain no legitimate expectations of privacy in their cells, but it goes almost without saying that "[t]he prisoner and the schoolchild stand in wholly different circumstances, separated by the harsh facts of criminal conviction and incarceration" [*Ingraham*]. We are not yet ready to hold that the schools and the prisons need be equated for purposes of the Fourth Amendment. . . .

Against the child's interest in privacy must be set the substantial interest of teachers and administrators in maintaining discipline in the classroom and on school grounds. Maintaining order in the classroom has never been easy, but in recent years, school disorder has often taken particularly ugly forms: drug use and violent crime in the schools have become major social problems. Even in schools that have been spared the most severe disciplinary problems, the preservation of order and a proper educational environment requires close supervision of schoolchildren, as well as the enforcement of rules against conduct that would be perfectly permissible if undertaken by an adult. "Events calling for discipline are frequent occurrences and sometimes require immediate, effective action" [*Goss v. Lopez* (1975)]. Accordingly, we have recognized that maintaining security and order in the schools requires a certain degree of flexibility in school disciplinary procedures, and we have respected the value of preserving the informality of the student-teacher relationship.

A Standard of Reasonableness

How, then, should we strike the balance between the school-child's legitimate expectations of privacy and the school's equally legitimate need to maintain an environment in which learning can take place? It is evident that the school setting requires some easing of the restrictions to which searches by public authorities are ordinarily subject. The warrant requirement, in particular, is unsuited to the school environment: requiring a teacher to obtain a warrant before searching a child suspected of an infraction of school rules (or of the criminal law) would unduly interfere with the maintenance of the swift and informal disciplinary procedures needed in the schools. Just as we have in other cases dispensed with the warrant requirement when "the burden of obtaining a warrant is likely to frustrate the governmental purpose behind the search" [*Camara*], we hold today that school officials need not obtain a warrant before searching a student who is under their authority.

The school setting also requires some modification of the level of suspicion of illicit activity needed to justify a search. Ordinarily, a search—even one that may permissibly be carried out without a warrant—must be based upon "probable cause" to believe that a violation of the law has occurred. . . .

We join the majority of courts that have examined this issue in concluding that the accommodation of the privacy interests of schoolchildren with the substantial need of teachers and administrators for freedom to maintain order in the schools does not require strict adherence to the requirement that searches be based on probable cause to believe that the subject of the search has violated or is violating the law. Rather, the legality of a search of a student should depend simply on the reasonableness, under all the circumstances, of the search. Determining the reasonableness of any search involves a twofold inquiry: first, one must consider "whether the . . . action was justified at its inceptions" [*Terry v. Ohio* (1968)]; second, one must determine whether the search as actually conducted "was reasonably related in scope to the circumstances which justified the interference in the first place." Under ordinary circumstances, a search of a student by a teacher or other school official will be "justified at its inception" when there are reasonable grounds for suspecting that the search will turn up evidence that the student has violated or is violating either the law or the rules of the school. Such a search will be permissible in its scope when the measures adopted are reasonably related to the objectives of the search and not excessively intrusive in light of the age and sex of the student and the nature of the infraction.

This standard will, we trust, neither unduly burden the efforts of school authorities to maintain order in their schools nor authorize unrestrained intrusions upon the privacy of schoolchildren. By focusing attention on the question of reasonableness, the standard will spare teachers and school administrators the necessity of schooling themselves in the niceties of probable cause and permit them to regulate their conduct according to the dictates of reason and common sense. At the same time, the reasonableness standard should ensure that the interests of students will be invaded no more than is necessary to achieve the legitimate end of preserving order in the schools.

The Search of T.L.O.'s Purse

There remains the question of the legality of the search in this case. . . .

The incident that gave rise to this case actually involved two separate searches, with the first—the search for cigarettes—providing the suspicion that gave rise to the second—the search for marihuana. Although it is the fruits of the second search that are at issue here, the validity of the search for marihuana must depend on the reasonableness of the initial search for cigarettes, as there would have been no reason to suspect that T.L.O. possessed marihuana had the first search not taken place. Accordingly, it is to the search for cigarettes that we first turn our attention.

The New Jersey Supreme Court pointed to two grounds for its holding that the search for cigarettes was unreasonable. First, the court observed that possession of cigarettes was not in itself illegal or a violation of school rules. Because the contents of T.L.O.'s purse would therefore have "no direct bearing on the infraction" of which she was accused (smoking in a lavatory where smoking was prohibited), there was no reason to search her purse. Second, even assuming that a search of T.L.O.'s purse might under some circumstances be reasonable in light of the accusation made against T.L.O., the New Jersey court concluded that Mr. Choplick in this particular case had no reasonable grounds to suspect that T.L.O. had cigarettes in her purse. At best, according to the court, Mr. Choplick had "a good hunch."

Both these conclusions are implausible. T.L.O. had been accused of smoking, and had denied the accusation in the strongest possible terms when she stated that she did not smoke at all. Surely it cannot be said that under these circumstances, T.L.O.'s possession of cigarettes would be irrelevant to the charges against her or to her response to those charges. T.L.O.'s possession of cigarettes, once it was discovered, would both corroborate the report that she had been smoking and undermine the credibility of her defense to the charge of smoking. To be sure, the discovery of the cigarettes would not prove that T.L.O. had been smoking in the lavatory; nor would it, strictly speaking, necessarily be inconsistent with her claim that she did not smoke at all. . . .

Because the hypothesis that T.L.O. was carrying cigarettes in her purse was itself not unreasonable, it is irrelevant that other hypotheses were also consistent with the teacher's accusation. Accordingly, it cannot be said that Mr. Choplick acted unreasonably when he examined T.L.O.'s purse to see if it contained cigarettes.

Our conclusion that Mr. Choplick's decision to open T.L.O.'s purse was reasonable brings us to the question of the further search for marihuana once the pack of cigarettes was located. The suspicion upon which the search for marihuana was founded was provided when Mr. Choplick observed a package of rolling papers in the purse as he removed the pack of cigarettes. Although T.L.O. does not dispute the reasonableness of Mr. Choplick's belief that the rolling papers indicated the presence of marihuana, she does contend that the scope of the search Mr. Choplick conducted exceeded permissible bounds when he seized and read certain letters that implicated T.L.O. in drug dealing. This argument, too, is unpersuasive. The discovery of the rolling papers concededly gave rise to a reasonable suspicion that T.L.O. was carrying marihuana as well as cigarettes in her purse. This suspicion justified further exploration of T.L.O.'s purse, which turned up more evidence of drug-related activities: a pipe, a number of plastic bags of the type commonly used to store marihuana, a small quantity of marihuana, and a fairly substantial amount of money. Under these circumstances, it was not unreasonable to extend the search to a separate zippered compartment of the purse; and when a search of that compartment revealed an index card containing a list of "people who owe me money" as well as two letters, the inference that T.L.O. was involved in marihuana trafficking was substantial enough to justify Mr. Choplick in examining the letters to determine whether they contained any further evidence. In short, we cannot conclude that the search for marihuana was unreasonable in any respect.

Because the search resulting in the discovery of the evidence of marihuana dealing by T.L.O. was reasonable, the New Jersey Supreme Court's decision to exclude that evidence from T.L.O.'s juvenile delinquency proceedings on Fourth Amendment grounds was erroneous.

> "Students who voluntarily participate in
> school athletics have reason to expect
> intrusions upon normal rights and
> privileges, including privacy."

Schools May Test Students Involved in Athletics for Drugs

The Supreme Court's Decision

Antonin Scalia

In the following viewpoint, a US Supreme Court justice argues that public schools can require student athletes to submit to drug testing without violating their constitutional rights. The author notes that the Fourth Amendment's guarantee of an expectation of privacy against unreasonable searches is balanced by the interests of school officials to maintain order. He claims that students, particularly student athletes, have a reduced expectation of privacy in the school setting. Given the strength of the government interest in deterring drug use along with students' limited expectation of privacy, he argues, the constitutional rights of student athletes are not violated by mandatory drug testing. Antonin Scalia has been an associate justice of the US Supreme Court since 1986.

Antonin Scalia, Majority opinion, *Vernonia School District 47J v. Acton*, United States Supreme Court, June 26, 1995.

Vernonia School District 47J (District) operates one high school and three grade schools in the logging community of Vernonia, Oregon. As elsewhere in small-town America, school sports play a prominent role in the town's life, and student athletes are admired in their schools and in the community.

A Drug-Testing Program

Drugs had not been a major problem in Vernonia schools. In the mid-to-late 1980's, however, teachers and administrators observed a sharp increase in drug use. Students began to speak out about their attraction to the drug culture, and to boast that there was nothing the school could do about it. Along with more drugs came more disciplinary problems. Between 1988 and 1989 the number of disciplinary referrals in Vernonia schools rose to more than twice the number reported in the early 1980's, and several students were suspended. Students became increasingly rude during class; outbursts of profane language became common.

Not only were student athletes included among the drug users but, as the District Court found, athletes were the leaders of the drug culture. This caused the District's administrators particular concern, since drug use increases the risk of sports-related injury. Expert testimony at the trial confirmed the deleterious effects of drugs on motivation, memory, judgment, reaction, coordination, and performance. The high school football and wrestling coach witnessed a severe sternum injury suffered by a wrestler, and various omissions of safety procedures and misexecutions by football players, all attributable in his belief to the effects of drug use.

Initially, the District responded to the drug problem by offering special classes, speakers, and presentations designed to deter drug use. It even brought in a specially trained dog to detect drugs, but the drug problem persisted. According to the District Court:

> [T]he administration was at its wits end and . . . a large segment of the student body, particularly those involved in

interscholastic athletics, was in a state of rebellion. Disciplinary actions had reached 'epidemic proportions.' The coincidence of an almost three-fold increase in classroom disruptions and disciplinary reports along with the staff's direct observations of students using drugs or glamorizing drug and alcohol use led the administration to the inescapable conclusion that the rebellion was being fueled by alcohol and drug abuse as well as the student's misperceptions about the drug culture.

At that point, District officials began considering a drug-testing program. They held a parent "input night" to discuss the proposed Student Athlete Drug Policy (Policy), and the parents in attendance gave their unanimous approval. The school board approved the Policy for implementation in the fall of 1989. Its expressed purpose is to prevent student athletes from using drugs, to protect their health and safety, and to provide drug users with assistance programs.

The Student Athlete Drug Policy

The Policy applies to all students participating in interscholastic athletics. Students wishing to play sports must sign a form consenting to the testing and must obtain the written consent of their parents. Athletes are tested at the beginning of the season for their sport. In addition, once each week of the season the names of the athletes are placed in a "pool" from which a student, with the supervision of two adults, blindly draws the names of 10% of the athletes for random testing. Those selected are notified and tested that same day, if possible.

The student to be tested completes a specimen control form which bears an assigned number. Prescription medications that the student is taking must be identified by providing a copy of the prescription or a doctor's authorization. The student then enters an empty locker room accompanied by an adult monitor of the same sex. Each boy selected produces a sample at a urinal, remaining fully clothed with his back to the monitor, who stands approximately 12 to 15 feet behind the student. Monitors

TEENAGE DRUG USE

Percent who used any illicit drug in lifetime

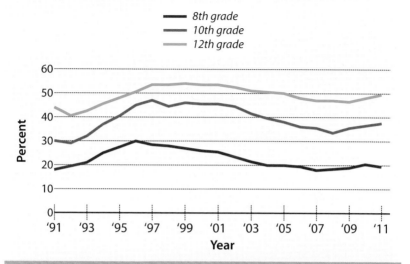

Taken from: Lloyd D. Johnson, Patrick M. O'Malley, Jerald G. Bachman, and John E. Schulenberg, *Monitoring the Future National Results on Adolescent Drug Use: Overview of Key Findings, 2011.* Ann Arbor: Institute for Social Research, University of Michigan, 2012.

may (though do not always) watch the student while he produces the sample, and they listen for normal sounds of urination. Girls produce samples in an enclosed bathroom stall, so that they can be heard but not observed. After the sample is produced, it is given to the monitor, who checks it for temperature and tampering and then transfers it to a vial.

The samples are sent to an independent laboratory, which routinely tests them for amphetamines, cocaine, and marijuana. Other drugs, such as LSD, may be screened at the request of the District, but the identity of a particular student does not determine which drugs will be tested. The laboratory's procedures are 99.94% accurate. The District follows strict procedures regarding the chain of custody and access to test results. The laboratory does not know the identity of the students whose samples it tests. It is authorized to mail written test reports only to the superintendent and to provide test results to District personnel by telephone only after the requesting official recites a code confirming his authority. Only the superintendent, principals, vice-principals, and athletic directors have access to test results, and the results are not kept for more than one year.

If a sample tests positive, a second test is administered as soon as possible to confirm the result. If the second test is negative, no further action is taken. If the second test is positive, the athlete's parents are notified, and the school principal convenes a meeting with the student and his parents, at which the student is given the option of (1) participating for six weeks in an assistance program that includes weekly urinalysis, or (2) suffering suspension from athletics for the remainder of the current season and the next athletic season. The student is then retested prior to the start of the next athletic season for which he or she is eligible. The Policy states that a second offense results in automatic imposition of option (2); a third offense in suspension for the remainder of the current season and the next two athletic seasons.

In the fall of 1991, respondent James Acton, then a seventh grader, signed up to play football at one of the District's grade schools. He was denied participation, however, because he and his parents refused to sign the testing consent forms. The Actons filed suit, seeking declaratory and injunctive relief from enforcement of the Policy on the grounds that it violated the Fourth and Fourteenth Amendments to the United States Constitution. . . .

The Fourth Amendment

The Fourth Amendment to the United States Constitution provides that the Federal Government shall not violate "[t]he right of the people to be secure in their persons, houses, papers, and effects, against unreasonable searches and seizures. . . ." We have held that the Fourteenth Amendment extends this constitutional guarantee to searches and seizures by state officers, including public school officials. In *Skinner v. Railway Labor Executives'*

Assn. (1989), we held that state-compelled collection and testing of urine, such as that required by the Policy, constitutes a "search" subject to the demands of the Fourth Amendment.

As the text of the Fourth Amendment indicates, the ultimate measure of the constitutionality of a governmental search is "reasonableness." At least in a case such as this, where there was no clear practice, either approving or disapproving the type of search at issue, at the time the constitutional provision was enacted, whether a particular search meets the reasonableness standard "'is judged by balancing its intrusion on the individual's Fourth Amendment interests against its promotion of legitimate governmental interests'" [*Skinner*, quoting *Delaware v. Prouse* (1979)]. Where a search is undertaken by law enforcement officials to discover evidence of criminal wrongdoing, this Court has said that reasonableness generally requires the obtaining of a judicial warrant. Warrants cannot be issued, of course, without the showing of probable cause required by the Warrant Clause. But a warrant is not required to establish the reasonableness of *all* government searches; and when a warrant is not required (and the Warrant Clause therefore not applicable), probable cause is not invariably required either. A search unsupported by probable cause can be constitutional, we have said, "when special needs, beyond the normal need for law enforcement, make the warrant and probable-cause requirement impracticable" [*Griffin v. Wisconsin* (1987)].

We have found such "special needs" to exist in the public school context. There, the warrant requirement "would unduly interfere with the maintenance of the swift and informal disciplinary procedures [that are] needed," and "strict adherence to the requirement that searches be based on probable cause" would undercut "the substantial need of teachers and administrators for freedom to maintain order in the schools" [*New Jersey v. T.L.O.* (1985)]. The school search we approved in *T.L.O.*, while not based on probable cause, *was* based on individualized *suspicion* of wrongdoing. As we explicitly acknowledged, however,

In 1995 the US Supreme Court ruled that drug testing for players on high school teams was constitutional. © Erik Isakson/Blend Images/Getty Images.

"'the Fourth Amendment imposes no irreducible requirement of such suspicion.'" We have upheld suspicionless searches and seizures to conduct drug testing of railroad personnel involved in train accidents; to conduct random drug testing of federal customs officers who carry arms or are involved in drug interdiction; and to maintain automobile checkpoints looking for illegal immigrants and contraband, and drunk drivers.

Expectations of Privacy at School

The first factor to be considered is the nature of the privacy interest upon which the search here at issue intrudes. The Fourth Amendment does not protect all subjective expectations of privacy, but only those that society recognizes as "legitimate." What expectations are legitimate varies, of course, with context, depending, for example, upon whether the individual asserting the privacy interest is at home, at work, in a car, or in a public park. In addition, the legitimacy of certain privacy expectations vis-à-vis the State may depend upon the individual's legal relationship with the State. For example, in *Griffin* [*v. Wisconsin* (1987)], we held that, although a "probationer's home, like anyone else's, is protected by the Fourth Amendmen[t]," the supervisory relationship between probationer and State justifies "a degree of impingement upon [a probationer's] privacy that would not be constitutional if applied to the public at large." Central, in our view, to the present case is the fact that the subjects of the Policy are (1) children, who (2) have been committed to the temporary custody of the State as schoolmaster.

Traditionally at common law, and still today, unemancipated minors lack some of the most fundamental rights of self-determinations—including even the right of liberty in its narrow sense, *i.e.*, the right to come and go at will. They are subject, even as to their physical freedom, to the control of their parents or guardians. When parents place minor children in private schools for their education, the teachers and administrators of those schools stand *in loco parentis* [in the place of a parent] over the children entrusted to them. . . .

Fourth Amendment rights, no less than First and Fourteenth Amendment rights, are different in public schools than elsewhere; the "reasonableness" inquiry cannot disregard the schools' custodial and tutelary responsibility for children. For their own good and that of their classmates, public school children are routinely required to submit to various physical examinations, and to be vaccinated against various diseases. . . .

Legitimate privacy expectations are even less with regard to student athletes. School sports are not for the bashful. They require "suiting up" before each practice or event, and showering and changing afterwards. Public school locker rooms, the usual sites for these activities, are not notable for the privacy they afford. The locker rooms in Vernonia are typical: No individual dressing rooms are provided; shower heads are lined up along a wall, unseparated by any sort of partition or curtain; not even all the toilet stalls have doors. As the United States Court of Appeals for the Seventh Circuit has noted, there is "an element of 'communal undress' inherent in athletic participation" [*Schaill by Kross v. Tippecanoe County School Corp.* (1988)].

There is an additional respect in which school athletes have a reduced expectation of privacy. By choosing to "go out for the team," they voluntarily subject themselves to a degree of regulation even higher than that imposed on students generally. In Vernonia's public schools, they must submit to a preseason physical exam (James testified that his included the giving of a urine sample), they must acquire adequate insurance coverage or sign an insurance waiver, maintain a minimum grade point average, and comply with any "rules of conduct, dress, training hours and related matters as may be established for each sport by the head coach and athletic director with the principal's approval." Somewhat like adults who choose to participate in a "closely regulated industry," students who voluntarily participate in school athletics have reason to expect intrusions upon normal rights and privileges, including privacy.

The Invasiveness of Drug Testing

Having considered the scope of the legitimate expectation of privacy at issue here, we turn next to the character of the intrusion that is complained of. We recognized in *Skinner* [*v. Railway Labor Executive's Association* (1989)] that collecting the samples for urinalysis intrudes upon "an excretory function traditionally shielded by great privacy." We noted, however, that the degree of intrusion depends upon the manner in which production of the urine sample is monitored. Under the District's Policy, male students produce samples at a urinal along a wall. They remain fully clothed and are only observed from behind, if at all. Female students produce samples in an enclosed stall, with a female monitor standing outside listening only for sounds of tampering. These conditions are nearly identical to those typically encountered in public restrooms, which men, women, and especially schoolchildren use daily. Under such conditions, the privacy interests compromised by the process of obtaining the urine sample are in our view negligible.

The other privacy-invasive aspect of urinalysis is, of course, the information it discloses concerning the state of the subject's body, and the materials he has ingested. In this regard it is significant that the tests at issue here look only for drugs, and not for whether the student is, for example, epileptic, pregnant, or diabetic. Moreover, the drugs for which the samples are screened are standard, and do not vary according to the identity of the student. And finally, the results of the tests are disclosed only to a limited class of school personnel who have a need to know; and they are not turned over to law enforcement authorities or used for any internal disciplinary function. . . .

The Governmental Concern

Finally, we turn to consider the nature and immediacy of the governmental concern at issue here, and the efficacy of this means for meeting it. In both *Skinner* and [*National Treasury Employees Union v. Von Raab* (1989)], we characterized the government interest motivating the search as "compelling." . . .

It is a mistake, however, to think that the phrase "compelling state interest," in the Fourth Amendment context, describes a fixed, minimum quantum of governmental concern, so that one can dispose of a case by answering in isolation the question: Is there a compelling state interest here? Rather, the phrase describes an interest that appears *important enough* to justify the particular search at hand, in light of other factors that show the search to be relatively intrusive upon a genuine expectation of privacy. Whether that relatively high degree of government concern is necessary in this case or not, we think it is met.

That the nature of the concern is important—indeed, perhaps compelling—can hardly be doubted. Deterring drug use by our Nation's schoolchildren is at least as important as enhancing efficient enforcement of the Nation's laws against the importation of drugs, which was the governmental concern in *Von Raab*, or deterring drug use by engineers and trainmen, which was the governmental concern in *Skinner*. School years are the time when the physical, psychological, and addictive effects of drugs are most severe. . . . And of course the effects of a drug-infested school are visited not just upon the users, but upon the entire student body and faculty, as the educational process is disrupted. In the present case, moreover, the necessity for the State to act is magnified by the fact that this evil is being visited not just upon individuals at large, but upon children for whom it has undertaken a special responsibility of care and direction. Finally, it must not be lost sight of that this program is directed more narrowly to drug use by school athletes, where the risk of immediate physical harm to the drug user or those with whom he is playing his sport is particularly high. Apart from psychological effects, which include impairment of judgment, slow reaction time, and a lessening of the perception of pain, the particular drugs screened by the District's Policy have been demonstrated to pose substantial physical risks to athletes. . . .

Taking into account all the factors we have considered above—the decreased expectation of privacy, the relative unobtrusiveness of the search, and the severity of the need met by the search—we conclude Vernonia's Policy is reasonable and hence constitutional.

> *"We find that testing students who participate in extracurricular activities is a reasonably effective means of addressing the School District's legitimate concerns in preventing, deterring, and detecting drug use."*

Schools May Test Students Involved in Extracurricular Activities for Drugs

The Supreme Court's Decision

Clarence Thomas

In the following viewpoint, a US Supreme Court justice argues that a school policy of drug testing students involved in extracurricular activities is constitutional. The author contends that a student's privacy interest in public school is limited, especially for students who participate in extracurricular activities. He concludes that the limited privacy students have at school, coupled with the school's legitimate interest in curbing drug use, supports the constitutionality of a school policy requiring drug testing for students involved in extracurricular activities. Clarence Thomas has been an associate justice of the US Supreme Court since 1991.

Clarence Thomas, Majority opinion, *Board of Education v. Earls*, United States Supreme Court, June 27, 2002.

The Student Activities Drug Testing Policy implemented by the Board of Education of Independent School District No. 92 of Pottawatomie County (School District) requires all students who participate in competitive extracurricular activities to submit to drug testing. Because this Policy reasonably serves the School District's important interest in detecting and preventing drug use among its students, we hold that it is constitutional.

The city of Tecumseh, Oklahoma, is a rural community located approximately 40 miles southeast of Oklahoma City. The School District administers all Tecumseh public schools. In the fall of 1998, the School District adopted the Student Activities Drug Testing Policy (Policy), which requires all middle and high school students to consent to drug testing in order to participate in any extracurricular activity. In practice, the Policy has been applied only to competitive extracurricular activities sanctioned by the Oklahoma Secondary Schools Activities Association, such as the Academic Team, Future Farmers of America, Future Homemakers of America, band, choir, pom pon, cheerleading, and athletics. Under the Policy, students are required to take a drug test before participating in an extracurricular activity, must submit to random drug testing while participating in that activity, and must agree to be tested at any time upon reasonable suspicion. The urinalysis tests are designed to detect only the use of illegal drugs, including amphetamines, marijuana, cocaine, opiates, and barbituates, not medical conditions or the presence of authorized prescription medications.

Drug Testing and the Fourth Amendment

At the time of their suit, both respondents attended Tecumseh High School. Respondent Lindsay Earls was a member of the show choir, the marching band, the Academic Team, and the National Honor Society. Respondent Daniel James sought to participate in the Academic Team. Together with their parents, Earls and James brought a 42 U.S.C. §1983 action [civil action for deprivation of rights] against the School District, challenging the Policy both on its face and as applied to their participation in extracurricular activities. They alleged that the Policy violates the Fourth Amendment as incorporated by the Fourteenth Amendment and requested injunctive and declarative relief. They also argued that the School District failed to identify a special need for testing students who participate in extracurricular activities, and that the "Drug Testing Policy neither addresses a proven problem nor promises to bring any benefit to students or the school." . . .

The Fourth Amendment to the United States Constitution protects "[t]he right of the people to be secure in their persons, houses, papers, and effects, against unreasonable searches and seizures." Searches by public school officials, such as the collection of urine samples, implicate Fourth Amendment interests. We must therefore review the School District's Policy for "reasonableness," which is the touchstone of the constitutionality of a governmental search. . . .

Significantly, this Court has previously held that "special needs" inhere in the public school context. While schoolchildren do not shed their constitutional rights when they enter the schoolhouse, "Fourth Amendment rights . . . are different in public schools than elsewhere; the 'reasonableness' inquiry cannot disregard the schools' custodial and tutelary responsibility for children" [*Vernonia School District 47J v. Acton* (1995)]. In particular, a finding of individualized suspicion may not be necessary when a school conducts drug testing.

In *Vernonia*, this Court held that the suspicionless drug testing of athletes was constitutional. The Court, however, did not simply authorize all school drug testing, but rather conducted a fact-specific balancing of the intrusion on the children's Fourth Amendment rights against the promotion of legitimate governmental interests. Applying the principles of *Vernonia* to the somewhat different facts of this case, we conclude that Tecumseh's Policy is also constitutional.

Students' Privacy Interests

We first consider the nature of the privacy interest allegedly compromised by the drug testing. As in *Vernonia*, the context of the public school environment serves as the backdrop for the analysis of the privacy interest at stake and the reasonableness of the drug testing policy in general.

A student's privacy interest is limited in a public school environment where the State is responsible for maintaining discipline, health, and safety. Schoolchildren are routinely required to submit to physical examinations and vaccinations against disease. Securing order in the school environment sometimes requires that students be subjected to greater controls than those appropriate for adults.

Respondents argue that because children participating in nonathletic extracurricular activities are not subject to regular physicals and communal undress, they have a stronger expectation of privacy than the athletes tested in *Vernonia*. This distinction, however, was not essential to our decision in *Vernonia*, which depended primarily upon the school's custodial responsibility and authority.

In any event, students who participate in competitive extracurricular activities voluntarily subject themselves to many of the same intrusions on their privacy as do athletes. Some of these clubs and activities require occasional off-campus travel and communal undress. All of them have their own rules and requirements for participating students that do not apply to the student body as a whole. For example, each of the competitive extracurricular activities governed by the Policy must abide by the rules of the Oklahoma Secondary Schools Activities Association, and a faculty sponsor monitors the students for compliance with the various rules dictated by the clubs and activities. This regulation of extracurricular activities further diminishes the expectation of privacy among schoolchildren. We therefore conclude that the students affected by this Policy have a limited expectation of privacy.

The US Supreme Court has ruled that extracurricular activities such as marching band are subject to some of the same privacy limitations as athletics because students volunteer to participate. © Gary Conner/Photolibrary/Getty Images.

The Policy's Invasion of Privacy

Next, we consider the character of the intrusion imposed by the Policy. Urination is "an excretory function traditionally shielded by great privacy" [*Skinner v. Railway Labor Executive's Association* (1989)]. But the "degree of intrusion" on one's privacy caused by collecting a urine sample "depends upon the manner in which production of the urine sample is monitored" [*Vernonia*].

Under the Policy, a faculty monitor waits outside the closed restroom stall for the student to produce a sample and must "listen for the normal sounds of urination in order to guard against tampered specimens and to insure an accurate chain of custody." The monitor then pours the sample into two bottles that are sealed and placed into a mailing pouch along with a consent form signed by the student. This procedure is virtually identical to that reviewed in *Vernonia*, except that it additionally protects privacy by allowing male students to produce their samples behind a closed stall. Given that we considered the method of collection in *Vernonia* a "negligible" intrusion, the method here is even less problematic.

In addition, the Policy clearly requires that the test results be kept in confidential files separate from a student's other educational records and released to school personnel only on a "need to know" basis. Respondents nonetheless contend that the intrusion on students' privacy is significant because the Policy fails to protect effectively against the disclosure of confidential information and, specifically, that the school "has been careless in protecting that information: for example, the Choir teacher looked at students' prescription drug lists and left them where other students could see them." But the choir teacher is someone with a "need to know," because during off-campus trips she needs to know what medications are taken by her students. Even before the Policy was enacted the choir teacher had access to this information. In any event, there is no allegation that any other student did see such information. This one example of alleged carelessness hardly increases the character of the intrusion.

Moreover, the test results are not turned over to any law enforcement authority. Nor do the test results here lead to the imposition of discipline or have any academic consequences. Rather, the only consequence of a failed drug test is to limit the student's privilege of participating in extracurricular activities. Indeed, a student may test positive for drugs twice and still be allowed to participate in extracurricular activities. After the first positive test, the school contacts the student's parent or guardian for a meeting. The student may continue to participate in the activity if within five days of the meeting the student shows proof of receiving drug counseling and submits to a second drug test in two weeks. For the second positive test, the student is suspended from participation in all extracurricular activities for 14 days, must complete four hours of substance abuse counseling, and must submit to monthly drug tests. Only after a third positive test will the student be suspended from participating in any extracurricular activity for the remainder of the school year, or 88 school days, whichever is longer.

Given the minimally intrusive nature of the sample collection and the limited uses to which the test results are put, we conclude that the invasion of students' privacy is not significant.

The Government's Concerns

Finally, this Court must consider the nature and immediacy of the government's concerns and the efficacy of the Policy in meeting them. This Court has already articulated in detail the importance of the governmental concern in preventing drug use by schoolchildren. The drug abuse problem among our Nation's youth has hardly abated since *Vernonia* was decided in 1995. In fact, evidence suggests that it has only grown worse. As in *Vernonia*, "the necessity for the State to act is magnified by the fact that this evil is being visited not just upon individuals at large, but upon children for whom it has undertaken a special responsibility of care and direction." The health and safety risks identified in *Vernonia* apply with equal force to Tecumseh's children. Indeed, the nationwide drug epidemic makes the war against drugs a pressing concern in every school.

Additionally, the School District in this case has presented specific evidence of drug use at Tecumseh schools. Teachers testified that they had seen students who appeared to be under the influence of drugs and that they had heard students speaking openly about using drugs. A drug dog found marijuana cigarettes near the school parking lot. Police officers once found drugs or drug paraphernalia in a car driven by a Future Farmers of America member. And the school board president reported that people in the community were calling the board to discuss the "drug situation." We decline to second-guess the finding of the District Court that "[v]iewing the evidence as a whole, it cannot be reasonably disputed that the [School District] was faced with a 'drug problem' when it adopted the Policy."

The Extensiveness of Student Drug Testing After *Earls*

It is estimated . . . that by May 2008, *at a minimum*, 16.5 percent (16.5%) of U.S. public school districts have student random drug-testing programs with a conservative estimated annual average increase, based upon current frequency levels, of at least one percent (1%) of districts adding these programs to existing prevention programs every year.

> *C.E. Edwards, "How Many Public School Districts Currently Test Students for Illicit Drugs on a Random Basis?," Drug-Free Projects Coalition, Inc., June 2008. www.studentdrugtesting.org.*

Respondents consider the proffered evidence insufficient and argue that there is no "real and immediate interest" to justify a policy of drug testing nonathletes. We have recognized, however, that "[a] demonstrated problem of drug abuse . . . [is] not in all cases necessary to the validity of a testing regime," but that some showing does "shore up an assertion of special need for a suspicionless general search program" [*Chandler v. Miller* (1997)]. The School District has provided sufficient evidence to shore up the need for its drug testing program.

Furthermore, this Court has not required a particularized or pervasive drug problem before allowing the government to conduct suspicionless drug testing. For instance, in [*National Treasury Employees Union v. Von Raab* (1989)] the Court upheld the drug testing of customs officials on a purely preventive basis, without any documented history of drug use by such officials. In response to the lack of evidence relating to drug use, the Court noted generally that "drug abuse is one of the most serious problems confronting our society today," and that programs to prevent and detect drug use among customs officials could not be deemed unreasonable. Likewise, the need to prevent and deter the substantial harm of childhood drug use provides the necessary immediacy for a school testing policy. Indeed, it would make little sense to require a school district to wait for substantial portion of its students to begin using drugs before it was allowed to institute a drug testing program designed to deter drug use.

Given the nationwide epidemic of drug use, and the evidence of increased drug use in Tecumseh schools, it was entirely reasonable for the School District to enact this particular drug testing policy. We reject the Court of Appeals' novel test that "any district seeking to impose a random suspicionless drug testing policy as a condition to participation in a school activity must demonstrate that there is some identifiable drug abuse problem among a sufficient number of those subject to the testing, such that testing that group of students will actually redress its drug problem." Among other problems, it would be difficult to administer such a test. As we cannot articulate a threshold level of drug use that would suffice to justify a drug testing program for schoolchildren, we refuse to fashion what would in effect be a constitutional quantum of drug use necessary to show a "drug problem."

A Reasonable Policy

Respondents also argue that the testing of nonathletes does not implicate any safety concerns, and that safety is a "crucial factor" in applying the special needs framework. They contend that there must be "surpassing safety interests" [*Skinner*], or "extraordinary safety and national security hazards" [*Von Raab*], in order to override the usual protections of the Fourth Amendment. Respondents are correct that safety factors into the special needs analysis, but the safety interest furthered by drug testing is undoubtedly substantial for all children, athletes and nonathletes alike. We know all too well that drug use carries a variety of health risks for children, including death from overdose.

We also reject respondents' argument that drug testing must presumptively be based upon an individualized reasonable suspicion of wrongdoing because such a testing regime would be less intrusive. In this context, the Fourth Amendment does not require a finding of individualized suspicion, and we decline to impose such a requirement on schools attempting to prevent and detect drug use by students. Moreover, we question whether testing based on individualized suspicion in fact would be less intrusive. Such a regime would place an additional burden on public school teachers who are already tasked with the difficult job of maintaining order and discipline. A program of individualized suspicion might unfairly target members of unpopular groups. The fear of lawsuits resulting from such targeted searches may chill enforcement of the program, rendering it ineffective in combating drug use. In any case, this Court has repeatedly stated that reasonableness under the Fourth Amendment does not require employing the least intrusive means, because "[t]he logic of such elaborate less-restrictive-alternative arguments could raise insuperable barriers to the exercise of virtually all search-and-seizure powers" [*United States v. Martinez-Fuerte* (1976)].

Finally, we find that testing students who participate in extracurricular activities is a reasonably effective means of addressing the School District's legitimate concerns in preventing, deterring, and detecting drug use. While in *Vernonia* there might have been a closer fit between the testing of athletes and the trial court's finding that the drug problem was "fueled by the 'role model' effect of athletes' drug use," such a finding was not essential to the holding. *Vernonia* did not require the school to test the group of students most likely to use drugs, but rather considered the constitutionality of the program in the context of the public school's custodial responsibilities. Evaluating the Policy in this context, we conclude that the drug testing of Tecumseh students who participate in extracurricular activities effectively serves the School District's interest in protecting the safety and health of its students.

Within the limits of the Fourth Amendment, local school boards must assess the desirability of drug testing schoolchildren. In upholding the constitutionality of the Policy, we express no opinion as to its wisdom. Rather, we hold only that Tecumseh's Policy is a reasonable means of furthering the School District's important interest in preventing and deterring drug use among its schoolchildren.

| *"This comes close to saying that high school kids have no Fourth Amendment rights."*

The Lawyer for the *Earls* Defendant Laments the Court's Decision

Personal Narrative

Graham Boyd, interviewed by Janelle Brown

In the following viewpoint, a journalist interviews the lawyer who represented students opposing drug testing in Board of Education v. Earls *(2002). The lawyer talks about his loss in the US Supreme Court and the impact it will have on student drug testing. He claims that student drug testing is an invasion of privacy and does not work to prevent drug use. He worries that the ruling in* Earls *has further limited the Fourth Amendment rights of students. Graham Boyd is a lawyer for the American Civil Liberties Union (ACLU) and founder of the ACLU Drug Law Reform Project. Janelle Brown is a novelist, essayist, and journalist.*

On Thursday [June 27, 2002], the Supreme Court ruled 5-4 in the case of the *Board of Education v. Earls* that it is "reasonable" under the Fourth Amendment to randomly administer drug tests to all high school students who participate in extracurricular activities. In other words, it is now perfectly legal for a school to force a cheerleader or the president of the chess club to pee in a cup—anytime—to keep their membership in after-school programs.

Reaction to the Ruling

The decision didn't come as a surprise. During oral arguments on the case in March, several Supreme Court justices expressed strong support for student drug testing. At one point, Justice Antonin Scalia taunted Graham Boyd, the ACLU [American Civil Liberties Union] lawyer who argued the case on behalf of defendant Lindsay Earls: "So long as you have a bunch of druggies who are orderly in class, the school can take no action. That's what you want us to rule?" At another juncture, Justice Anthony Kennedy asked Boyd a hypothetical question about whether a district could have two schools, one a "druggie school" and one with drug testing. As for the first, Justice Kennedy said, "no parent would send a child to that school, except maybe your client." (Earls, a former honor student at Tecumseh High School in Oklahoma, had objected to drug testing as an intrusion on her right to privacy.)

Even though they had anticipated defeat, opponents of the war on drugs—and its new battlefield in the classroom—found it deeply disappointing. These critics argue that by targeting students, particularly those who participate in extracurricular activities, be they athletes, prom queens or Future Farmers of America, participating schools unfairly single out students who are often the least likely to be doing drugs in the first place, and drive students at risk for drug use away from the activities that might take the place of getting high. Furthermore, they argue, drug testing erodes the privacy of high school students; and it has never proven to be an effective method of reducing drug use among kids.

Justice Clarence Thomas, who wrote the majority opinion for the case, clearly wasn't swayed by these arguments. "Students affected by this policy have a limited expectation of privacy," he wrote. "This policy reasonably serves the School District's important interest in detecting and preventing drug use among its students."

In an interview following the ruling, Boyd, who is the director of the ACLU Drug Policy Litigation Project, talked about the impact of the decision, which he believes will result in more drug testing in the nation's schools, and, perhaps more importantly, a serious erosion of constitutional rights to privacy for everyone—students and adults.

Janelle Brown: What's the message being sent by this ruling?

Graham Boyd: Basically, it's disappointing on a lot of levels. It certainly erodes students' privacy in a way that has never been done by the court before, and really puts students on par with prisoners. In his decision, Justice Thomas focuses almost dispositively on the fact that students are in what he calls the "custody of the school" and that drugs are themselves dangerous. There's no drug problem in this school in question, no safety issue . . . but the mere fact of being a student seems to be, in Thomas' opinion, a reason to drug-test.

The logic of the opinion is so different from Vernonia, Ore. [a previous US Supreme Court ruling that allowed drug testing of student athletes only]. In that case, there were a lot of reasons to uphold the drug testing: There was a drug problem in general, which was centered around athletes, who were school role models. This reason, and others, were absent in Tecumseh.

Drug Testing in Schools

Do you expect schools across the nation to immediately start or expand drug-testing programs?

The good news in this is that schools have not previously been that responsive to the Supreme Court on this issue. It's been seven years since the *Vernonia [School District 47J v. Acton* (1995)] decision, and still only 5 percent of all schools drug-test their athletes. Cost is one factor [drug tests cost upwards of $25 per person] but it's also a question of effectiveness. A newspaper reported yesterday that the Dublin, Ohio, school board decided to stop drug-testing students, saying that it was ineffective. They said they knew that the Supreme Court was about to rule on this issue, but they didn't care: They wanted to do what would actually help the kids.

I think it's not going to be a legal question for most schools; it's a question of what works. The politics around drug testing are very thick but the evidence of it actually *helping* anybody is absent. And most school boards are controlled by people who want to help kids, so they aren't going to go down this road.

So, you don't think many school districts were waiting for a Supreme Court go-ahead?

I haven't heard of a single school district that is doing this, but I'm sure they are out there. What invariably happens is a small number of parents start to make a lot of noise about needing to do something about drugs; and drug testing is an easy decision that shows that the school board is tough on drugs.

It's not that different from what Congress does with mandatory minimum sentencing: It's a cheap political gesture that keeps voters happy but in the cold light of day doesn't hold up [as a meaningful action]. No one thinks raising jail terms for crack possession is going to have an effect, but it gives them something to campaign on. Everyone knows that drug testing is at best a waste of money, but it makes [school boards] look good. . . .

Do you think the current Supreme Court would lean towards drug testing all students if the issue came up?

Attorney Graham Boyd, center, and Lindsey Earls, right, answer questions from reporters in front of the US Supreme Court building on March 19, 2002. © AP Images/Susan Walsh.

I think you've got to read a lot into Justice [Stephen] Breyer's [concurring] opinion. In one little paragraph he says that for the student who really doesn't want to [be tested] they could always just not participate in the extracurricular activities; and he acknowledges that this is a serious matter, but a very different matter than saying the kid would be expelled from school altogether.

That's really what it comes down to in the question of drug testing *all* students: What do you do with a kid who refuses to be tested? To say that a kid can't be in the choir if they refuse the test, that's harsh. But say that they can't get a public school education at all if they object? That's awful.

The Wisdom of Student Drug Testing

So, what recourse is there currently for extracurricular students who don't want to take this test? Do they have a leg to stand on?

You've got to look further down the road. Drug testing doesn't exist in most schools right now, and if schools want to do this they have to hold hearings and get input from the public. So it's important for students and parents to engage in that process, bring information into those meetings.

What's nice is this isn't just about people complaining about privacy; it's also about educating school boards that this kind of drug testing is counterproductive. That's a very empowering argument, and we're doing everything we can to really encourage students and their parents to exercise their own voice.

In the Supreme Court decision, though, Justice Thomas wrote that "testing students who participate in extracurricular activities is a reasonably effective means of addressing the school district's legitimate concerns in preventing, deterring and detecting drug use." Why did he write this? Is there, as he suggests, proof that it was reasonably effective?

Your guess is as good as mine: There is none. There really is no evidence whatsoever that drug testing is at all effective. The evidence is the opposite.

Thomas also suggested that the Supreme Court wasn't ruling that the decision to drug-test was "wise," just that it was constitutional.

It is affirmatively unwise, in the view of most experts. In a limited sense, one could read this as support of school-board discretion. I hope the boards will be responsible in use of that discretion.

The Rights of Students

What message does this decision send about student privacy rights? Is this essentially arguing that students have no Fourth Amendment rights anymore?

This comes close to saying that high school kids have no Fourth Amendment rights. It doesn't completely upset the balance, but it does suggest a drug-war exception in schools. Lower courts are going to be tempted to endorse any kind of anti-drug measure a school wants to take.

We'll fight that, it's not a foregone conclusion, but that's one of the dangers of today's decision.

What's the likelihood that these rights will ever be returned to high school students? Is this a slippery slope of privacy loss that is impossible to climb back up?

It's a huge concern. When the Supreme Court rules, it often remains precedent for a generation at least. And they've now set the bar very low for intrusions on student privacy in the name of the war on drugs.

Of equal concern for me is that what happens to young people in the privacy realm could also have an impact on the privacy rights of that generation when they come of age. One of the fundamental ways the Fourth Amendment is measured is by reasonable but subjective expectations of privacy: "Do I personally feel offended by this?" If I don't feel it's a big deal, the government can do it. To the extent that kids become accustomed to various intrusions on their privacy, because of drug policies, they have no standing to object to *other* intrusions as they get older.

What other long term impact do you believe this decision will have on kids?

I'm going to make a mischievous argument. I think that in some ways the best thing that government officials could do to bring an end to the war on drugs is continue this trend of cracking down on young people.

For every student who is drug-tested, for every student who has to prove her innocence by passing a drug test, you'll have one more student that questions the drug war. Every time they teach D.A.R.E. [Drug Abuse Resistance Education program] and teach lies to kids, you'll have one more kid that doesn't believe in the drug war. Needless and groundless drug testing of high school students is just taking one more step down the road of having people say we've had enough.

> *"Random drug testing of students is an ineffective, humiliating, invasive practice that undermines the relationships between pupils and staff and runs contrary to the principles of due process."*

Student Drug Testing Is Ineffective and Damaging

Paul Armentano

In the following viewpoint, a drug policy reform advocate discusses studies showing that student drug-testing programs in public schools have failed to reduce substance abuse. Furthermore, he suggests that some of the evidence supports the view that the programs may actually put teens at risk by encouraging greater risk-taking behaviors. The author questions why schools are continuing to subject students to this invasion of privacy when there are no benefits to drug testing. Paul Armentano is the deputy director of the National Organization for the Reform of Marijuana Laws (NORML) and co-author of the book Marijuana Is Safer: So Why Are We Driving People to Drink?

Between the years 2003 and 2008, the U.S. Department of Education awarded more than $36 million in taxpayer dollars to fund student drug-testing programs in public high schools,

Paul Armentano, "Student Drug Testing Doesn't Work," *Los Angeles Times*, August 29, 2011. Copyright © 2011 by Paul Armentano. All rights reserved. Reproduced by permission.

including several in Southern California. A study published this month [August 2011] in the *Journal of Youth and Adolescence* reveals that this was not money well spent.

Studies of School Drug-Testing Programs

An international team of researchers from universities in the United States, Israel and Australia assessed the impact of school drug-testing programs on a nationally representative sample of 943 high school students.

Investigators [Sharon R. Sznitman, Sally M. Dunlop, Priya Nalkur, Atika Khurana, and Daniel Romer] reported that the imposition of random drug-screening programs failed to reduce males' self-reported use of alcohol, tobacco or illicit drugs. Student drug-testing programs were associated with minor reductions in females' self-reported drug history, but only among women who attended schools with "positive" environments. By contrast, investigators found that the enactment of drug-testing programs in "negative" school environments was most likely to be associated with "harmful effects on female youth."

The study's authors concluded: "The current research expands on previous findings indicating that school drug testing does not in and of itself deter substance use. . . . [D]rug testing should not be undertaken as a stand-alone substance prevention effort and that improvements in school climate should be considered before implementing drug testing."

The study's conclusions were hardly surprising. Despite claims that student drug-testing programs represent a potential "silver bullet" in society's effort to reduce adolescent drug abuse, studies evaluating the effectiveness of such programs have consistently demonstrated the opposite.

In fact, a 2010 Department of Education study found that federally funded mandatory random student drug-screening programs fail to reduce rates of drug use among either the students tested or among the student body at large. Drug testing

The Lack of Evidence for a Valid Government Interest

Vernonia [*School District 47J v. Acton* (1995)], and [*Board of Education v.*] *Earls* [2002] unfettered any number of preexisting restraints on school districts to combat the Great War on Drugs with random student drug testing. They now see their powers as nearly limitless so long as courts accept, at face value, that searches are an effective weapon in that war. This truth is assumed, often by citation to the Court itself: "Finally, we find that testing students . . . is a reasonably effective means of addressing the School District's legitimate concerns in preventing, deterring, and detecting drug use" [*Earls*]. Unfortunately, the Court had no evidence before it to make such a factual finding, and the current research reveals there is no evidence to support the proposition that drug testing is an effective weapon in the war on drugs. Consequently, there is no factual basis for a reasonable guardian or tutor to administer such a test nor a factual basis for otherwise supporting any school district's government interest as defined by *Vernonia* and *Earls*. And without a valid government interest, there is no legal justification for allowing random student drug testing under the Fourth Amendment—much less any economic justification for all the federal, state, and local funds spent on such programs.

Susan P. Stuart, "When the Cure Is Worse than the Disease: Student Random Drug Testing and Its Empirical Failure," Valparaiso University Law Review, *vol. 44, no. 4, Summer 2010.*

"had no statistically significant impacts" upon participants' substance use, the study found. "For nonparticipants, there was no significant difference in self-reported substance use between the treatment and control schools," the authors added.

Similarly, a 2007 study published in the *Journal of Adolescent Health* concluded that student drug-testing programs do not

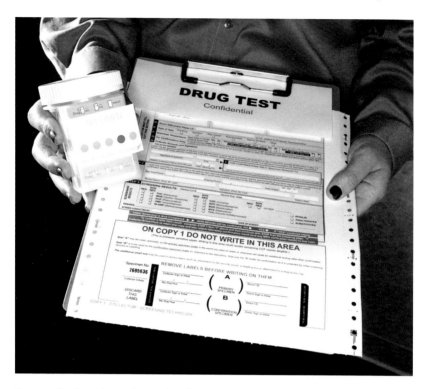

Some studies have shown that student drug testing is ineffective in preventing drug use and actually encourages at-risk behavior. © Jupiterimages/Comstock Images/Getty Images.

reduce self-reported drug use and may even encourage greater risk-taking behaviors among those tested. Investigators from Oregon's Health & Science University performed the two-year trial, which to date remains the only prospective randomized clinical trial to assess the deterrent effect of drug and alcohol testing among high school athletes.

Researchers found that students who underwent random drug testing did not differ in their self-reported drug use compared to students at neighboring schools who were not enrolled in drug-testing programs. Perhaps most disturbingly, researchers determined that students subjected to random drug testing were more likely to report an "increase in some risk factors for future substance use" compared to students who attended schools without drug and alcohol testing.

The Persistence of Drug-Testing Programs

Yet despite these programs' consistently poor performance, an estimated one-quarter of public schools now engage in some form of student drug testing. They shouldn't.

Random drug testing of students is an ineffective, humiliating, invasive practice that undermines the relationships between pupils and staff and runs contrary to the principles of due process. It compels teens to potentially submit evidence against themselves and forfeit their privacy rights as necessary requirements for attending school.

Rather than presuming our schoolchildren innocent of illicit activity, drug testing without suspicion presumes them guilty until they prove themselves innocent. Why are we continuing to send this message to our children?

> *"Thousands of schools are already conducting random student drug testing as part of ongoing efforts to promote a safe and healthy school environment."*

Student Drug Testing Is Effective and Does Not Violate Student Privacy

Office of National Drug Control Policy

In the following viewpoint, the Office of National Drug Control Policy (ONDCP) contends that many middle schools and high schools across the United States have successfully implemented student drug-testing programs. The ONDCP claims that a growing percentage of public and private schools now test their students for a variety of illicit drugs and sometimes for alcohol and nicotine. The ONDCP maintains that schools have created different strategies to implement drug testing in a way that protects student privacy. The Office of National Drug Control Policy advises the president on drug-control issues, coordinates drug-control activities, and produces the annual National Drug Control Strategy.

Just how many schools test students for drug use? Until recently, there has been very little national data on the prevalence of

Office of National Drug Control Policy, "CDC Study Indicates Thousands of Schools Have Random Testing Programs; Protecting Student Privacy," *Strategies for Success: New Pathways to Drug Abuse Prevention*, Summer–Fall 2008, vol. 1, no. 3, pp. 1–2, 6.

student drug testing. With no reliable mechanism to track random testing programs in public, private, and parochial schools, Federal estimates ranged from 500 to 2,000 and were based on the number of schools receiving U.S. Department of Education grants, results from surveys, and media reports. Then, in October 2007, the Centers for Disease Control and Prevention (CDC) released the results of a national survey, which contained questions related to student drug testing. Findings indicate that the number of schools conducting random testing may be closer to 4,000—more than double the highest estimates cited previously.

Student Drug Testing Nationwide

Every 6 years, the CDC conducts the School Health Policies and Programs Study (SHPPS) to gather data on the health and safety of students in public and private elementary, middle, and high schools across the country. The 2006 SHPPS is the largest and most comprehensive assessment of school health programs ever conducted in the United States, and it is the first one to include questions on student drug testing. SHPPS surveys teachers and administrators at the State, district, and school levels using computer-assisted telephone interviews, self-administered mail questionnaires, and computer-assisted personal interviews. Information was collected from all 50 States and the District of Columbia and included 461 school districts and 1,025 elementary, middle, and high schools. The survey sample was weighted to represent an estimated 125,333 schools nationwide.

Out of an estimated 59,364 middle and high schools in the country, weighted survey results from the individual schools included in the SHPPS suggest that 11.4 percent of middle schools and 19.5 percent of high schools include some type of drug testing as part of their drug-prevention programs. Approximately 7 percent of the public and private middle schools and high schools in the nation, or 4,200, conduct random student drug testing.

The study also shows that public and private schools test for similar drugs. Among the public and private middle and high

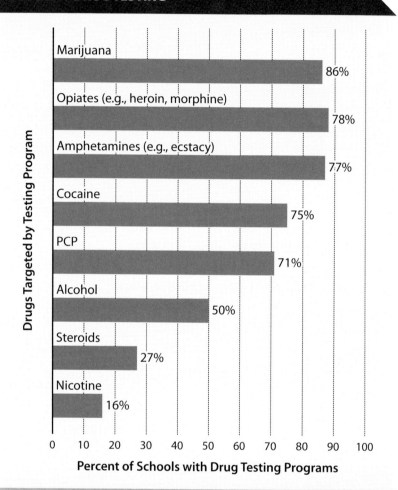

DRUGS TARGETED BY SCHOOLS CONDUCTING STUDENT DRUG TESTING

Drugs Targeted by Testing Program

- Marijuana — 86%
- Opiates (e.g., heroin, morphine) — 78%
- Amphetamines (e.g., ecstacy) — 77%
- Cocaine — 75%
- PCP — 71%
- Alcohol — 50%
- Steroids — 27%
- Nicotine — 16%

Percent of Schools with Drug Testing Programs

Taken from: Office of National Drug Control Policy, "CDC Study Indicates Thousands of Schools Have Random Testing Programs," *Strategies for Success: New Pathways to Drug Abuse Prevention*, vol. 1, no. 3, Summer–Fall 2008.

schools that conduct drug testing, 86 percent reported testing for marijuana, 78 percent tested for opiates (such as heroin or morphine), 77 percent tested for amphetamines (such as methamphetamine or ecstasy), 75 percent tested for cocaine, 71 percent tested for PCP, 50 percent tested for alcohol, 27 percent tested for steroids, and 16 percent tested for nicotine.

As for methods of testing, SHPPS determined that urine tests were most popular and were used by 84 percent of schools that tested. Forty percent of the schools reported using breathalyzer (breath alcohol) tests, 15 percent reported using hair tests, 8 percent reported using saliva tests, and 3 percent reported using sweat tests.

Almost all the middle and high schools that test have procedures in place to inform students and families about drug-testing and drug-use policies and what happens if a student violates school policy.

Also encouraging is the SHPPS finding that 72.2 percent of middle and high schools provided alcohol- or other drug-use treatment at schools through health services or mental health and social services staff, and 34.9 percent made arrangements for treatment through organizations or professionals outside of school.

Considerable progress has been made against youth drug and alcohol use. Today, 860,000 fewer young people are using drugs than in 2001. Yet researchers responsible for SHPPS caution, "more schools need to promote a positive school climate and reduce violence, injuries, and the use of tobacco, alcohol, and other substances." As the survey indicates, thousands of schools are already conducting random student drug testing as part of ongoing efforts to promote a safe and healthy school environment. . . .

Protecting Student Privacy

Testing begins and ends with privacy. Schools that conduct random student drug testing typically maintain privacy by restricting how many people have access to vital information, such as the identity and medical history of the student providing the sample, and the test results. However, privacy can be maintained in very different ways. The following describes two approaches to protecting student privacy during the random drug testing process.

At Hackettstown High School in Hackettstown, New Jersey, students selected for drug testing in the school's four-year-old testing program are called into the guidance office. A student may be summoned to the office for a variety of reasons, so little attention is paid to the half-dozen students who are called in each week for testing. When the student arrives, the guidance counselor escorts him or her to the school nurse's office. The student then provides a urine sample, which is tested immediately with a chemical test kit for the presence of prohibited substances.

If the on-site test is negative, the sample is destroyed. The only people aware of the test and the result are the student, the guidance counselor, and the school nurse.

If a sample tests positive, it is sent to a laboratory for a confirming test. A chain-of-custody form accompanies the sample. At this point, the student's name is not disclosed, and the laboratory knows the student only by a code number. If the test is confirmed positive, the results are sent to a medical review officer, who learns the student's identity through the guidance counselor.

Next, the medical review officer contacts the student's family to determine whether the student might be taking prescription medication under a physician's direction, possibly resulting in a nonnegative test. If this turns out to be the case, the medical review officer notifies the school's guidance counselor that the testing result is negative. The officer does not explain why the result was ruled negative, nor does he or she give out any information about which prescription drug may have been involved.

An Approach That Limits School Involvement

In North Carolina's Winston-Salem/Forsyth County School District, school personnel play no role in the district's random student drug testing program, which began in 1998. Rather, testing is conducted by a service agency hired by the district's Safe and Drug-Free Schools office. The contracting agency is a nonprofit

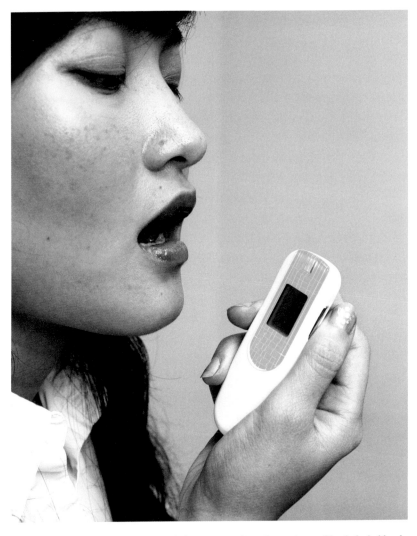

A young woman breathes into a Breathalyzer—a machine that estimates blood alcohol levels. While urinalysis is the most commonly used method, tests on breath, hair, saliva, and sweat are also administered in schools to test students for drug and alcohol use. © Gabriela Hasbun/ Aurora/Getty Images.

organization that provides treatment and education services related to mental health and substance abuse.

With this approach, technicians from the service agency arrive at the school without providing prior notice to the school. They randomly select students who are eligible for testing (students involved in athletics or other extracurricular activities, or who are voluntarily enrolled in the program). The agency collects the urine samples, establishes a chain-of-custody sequence, performs initial and confirmatory testing, and provides a medical review of results.

"The school knows the agency is there testing when the agency personnel show up, but the school is not involved in the process or know who is being tested," explained Mike Nesser, Program Specialist with the Winston-Salem/Forsyth County Schools Safe and Drug-Free School Office. "It takes a great deal of responsibility from school employees."

Samples are analyzed for seven compounds, and a separate steroid test may be administered to student athletes. Students are given the option of saliva testing if they cannot provide a urine sample, although in those cases the testing must be done off-site at the agency's facilities.

The service agency is responsible for contacting parents if more medical information is required or if any of the samples test positive. The agency also conducts counseling for students to assist them in recovery and in staying safe and drug free. At no time are the results, negative or positive, provided to school personnel. This way, said Nesser, school officials can spend more time educating students about the risks of alcohol and drug use.

Two school districts, two very different ways of ensuring privacy in drug testing. In both cases, access to the drug-testing information is limited to the student, his or her parents, and very few others. This policy allows the schools to ensure accurate, reliable results without jeopardizing students' privacy.

> *"Children are being acclimated to violations by the state that their grandparents would have found unconscionable."*

The Increased Acceptance Toward Student Drug Testing Threatens All

Peter Cassidy

In the following viewpoint, a writer argues that the growing acceptance of drug testing for students is likely to open the door for widespread drug testing both in and out of schools. The author claims that with drug testing limited at first to athletes, but later expanded to all students in extracurricular activities, it will not be long before it is considered fair to drug test all students. He expresses concern that the expansion of justifiable drug testing for students opens the door for the testing of adults in a variety of contexts. Peter Cassidy writes on national affairs, law, and technology.

In the past decade, a veritable *Kindergulag* [children's prison camp] has been erected around schoolchildren, making them subject to arbitrary curfews, physical searches, psychological profiling schemes and—in the latest institutionalized indignity—random, suspicion-less, warrant-less drug testing for just about any kid who wants to pursue extracurricular interests.

The Expansion of Student Drug Testing

Last summer, the Supreme Court gave *carte blanche* [unrestricted power] to school districts that want to impose drug testing on kids who've cast suspicion upon themselves by volunteering for extracurricular activities. The 5-to-4 decision [in *Board of Education v. Earls* (2002)] on June 27 upheld a drug-testing program in a Tecumseh County, Oklahoma, school district that requires students engaged in any "competitive" extracurricular activities to submit to random drug testing.

This isn't just about keeping jocks from enjoying a post-practice beer or joint. The decision approves the testing of any student who volunteers for the Future Farmers of America, Future Homemakers of America, the cheerleading squad, the choir, the color guard or even those sacrosanct curators of [US composer John Philip] Sousa, the marching band.

There is understandably a good deal of sympathy for drug testing as a social safety mechanism to catch kids who might be heading toward life-destroying drug abuse, social isolation and crime. Who doesn't want to catch a kid before he takes a life-long fall? Yet before parents surrender their kids to the arms of the therapeutic enforcement state, they need to come to terms with the provenance of the interventions they are tacitly endorsing for their kids—and some of the more enduring shared consequences of drug testing.

The History of Drug Testing

Drug testing actually arrived in American schools by way of the armed forces and the prison system. The Navy began testing servicemen for drugs 30 years ago, when the first test kits were developed. By the late '70s, prisoners were being subjected

Future Farmers of America (FFA) club members hold a Donkey Basketball fundraiser in their Arizona high school gym. US Supreme Court decisions allow students who belong to extracurricular clubs such as the FFA to be subjected to drug testing. © AP Images/Kingman Daily Minor/JC Amberlyn.

to urinalysis. By the mid-'80s, defense-related contractors were pressed to test their work forces for purity. In the final days of the [Ronald] Reagan administration, the Federal Drug Free Workplace Act forced drug testing on all federal contractors working on projects of any appreciable size. From there, against sporadic and fractured opposition by labor unions and civil liberties groups, urinalysis and drug-testing programs proliferated in almost every industry.

America's kids are now being subjected to the kind of intrusions the nation would inflict only upon conscripts and criminals just 20 or 30 years ago. Who knows how much further it could go? The latest decision in *Board of Education of Independent School District No. 92 v. Earls* essentially opens the way for general random drug testing of America's entire school population, says Timothy Lynch, director of the Criminal Justice Project at the Cato Institute in Washington.

The first movement toward urinalysis of the total student population was choreographed by the Supreme Court in 1995 with the *Vernonia School District v. Acton* case in Oregon. The court decided, among other things, that since athletes shower together, they have little expectation of privacy—and thus urinalysis of athletes was deemed constitutional.

In the case of Lindsay Earls—who was humiliated after being yanked out of choir practice by Tecumseh school administrators and ordered to urinate on command (she tested negative)—the Supreme Court justices appeared eager to extend the scope of drug testing. In oral arguments last March, Justice Anthony Kennedy taunted ACLU [American Civil Liberties Union] Attorney Graham Boyd, hypothesizing that his client would prefer to attend a "druggie" school.

Writing for the majority, Justice Clarence Thomas extended the relevance of the factors used to test "reasonableness" of a search in *Vernonia* to apply much more broadly, while enthroning the school district's interest in detecting drug use. In a breathtaking act of militant jurisprudence and shabby reasoning, Justice Thomas quickly expanded the universe of candidates for urinalysis and established a new entitlement for the state to determine the suitability of testing beyond parental guidance—"custodial responsibilities," he called it.

The Proliferation of Student Drug Testing Programs

After the decision, scores of school districts immediately began inspecting the language of the decision and considering establishing their own urinalysis programs based on the Tecumseh model.

In the Lockney School District in West Texas, Superintendent Raymond Lusk told the *New York Times* in September, "We'll probably get 85 percent of the kids in extracurriculars. I think

"It's for passing my drug test" cartoon by McCoy, Glenn and Gary, www.CartoonStock
.com. Copyright © McCoy, Glenn and Gary. Reproduction rights obtainable from www
.CartoonStock.com.

it would be fairer to test everybody, because why are some kids
more important than others?"

Touché. Now that there is a state entitlement to test at will,
pressing the PC [politically correct] buttons that demand fair-
ness in application of entitlements and social burdens will surely
extend testing to all students.

The prognosis for the rest of us is just as grim. With the Supreme Court establishing that the state has a superseding interest in cultivating a therapeutic enforcement role that trumps even clear, constitutionally guaranteed freedoms, nothing should be ruled out of the realm of possibility. A drug test requirement when you renew your driver's license? For filing a tax return? Before you vote?

Give it five years—or 50. Children are being acclimated to violations by the state that their grandparents would have found unconscionable. The future Supreme Court justices being conditioned in our schools today will no doubt chuckle in disbelief someday that on-demand urinalysis was ever an issue of legal contention.

10

"*The content of the suspicion failed to match the degree of intrusion.*"

It Is a Violation of Students' Rights for Schools to Conduct Unwarranted Searches

The Supreme Court's Decision

David Souter

In the following viewpoint, a US Supreme Court justice argues that although school officials have wide latitude in searching the clothing and possessions of students, strip searches are only justi- fied under extreme circumstances. The author contends that school officials need reasonable suspicion in order to search a student's outerwear and belongings, and this case warranted such a search. He concludes, however, that the suspicion was not strong enough to warrant an intrusive strip search of the student. David Souter served as an associate justice of the US Supreme Court from 1990 until his retirement in 2009.

David Souter, Majority opinion, *Safford Unified School District #1 v. Redding*, United States Supreme Court, June 25, 2009.

The issue here is whether a 13-year-old student's Fourth Amendment right was violated when she was subjected to a search of her bra and underpants by school officials acting on reasonable suspicion that she had brought forbidden prescription and over-the-counter drugs to school. Because there were no reasons to suspect the drugs presented a danger or were concealed in her underwear, we hold that the search did violate the Constitution. . . .

A Search of a Student

The events immediately prior to the search in question began in 13-year-old Savana Redding's math class at Safford Middle School one October day in 2003. The assistant principal of the school, Kerry Wilson, came into the room and asked Savana to go to his office. There, he showed her a day planner, unzipped and open flat on his desk, in which there were several knives, lighters, a permanent marker, and a cigarette. Wilson asked Savana whether the planner was hers; she said it was, but that a few days before she had lent it to her friend, Marissa Glines. Savana stated that none of the items in the planner belonged to her.

Wilson then showed Savana four white prescription-strength ibuprofen 400-mg pills, and one over-the-counter blue naproxen 200-mg pill, all used for pain and inflammation but banned under school rules without advance permission. He asked Savana if she knew anything about the pills. Savana answered that she did not. Wilson then told Savana that he had received a report that she was giving these pills to fellow students; Savana denied it and agreed to let Wilson search her belongings. Helen Romero, an administrative assistant, came into the office, and together with Wilson they searched Savana's backpack, finding nothing.

At that point, Wilson instructed Romero to take Savana to the school nurse's office to search her clothes for pills. Romero and the nurse, Peggy Schwallier, asked Savana to remove her jacket, socks, and shoes, leaving her in stretch pants and a T-shirt (both without pockets), which she was then asked to remove. Finally,

US Supreme Court Justice David H. Souter wrote the majority opinion in a case that ruled in favor of a student who was strip-searched by school officials. © David Hume Kennedy/Getty Images.

Savana was told to pull her bra out and to the side and shake it, and to pull out the elastic on her underpants, thus exposing her breasts and pelvic area to some degree. No pills were found.

Savana's mother filed suit against Safford Unified School District #1, Wilson, Romero, and Schwallier for conducting a strip search in violation of Savana's Fourth Amendment rights. . . .

A Standard of Reasonable Suspicion

The Fourth Amendment "right of the people to be secure in their persons . . . against unreasonable searches and seizures" generally requires a law enforcement officer to have probable cause for conducting a search. "Probable cause exists where 'the facts and circumstances within [an officer's] knowledge and of which [he] had reasonably trustworthy information [are] sufficient in themselves to warrant a man of reasonable caution in the belief that' an offense has been or is being committed" [*Brinegar v. United States* (1949), quoting *Carroll v. United States* (1925)], and that evidence bearing on that offense will be found in the place to be searched.

In [*New Jersey v.*] *T.L.O.* [1985], we recognized that the school setting "requires some modification of the level of suspicion of illicit activity needed to justify a search," and held that for searches by school officials "a careful balancing of governmental and private interests suggests that the public interest is best served by a Fourth Amendment standard of reasonableness that stops short of probable cause." We have thus applied a standard of reasonable suspicion to determine the legality of a school administrator's search of a student, and have held that a school search "will be permissible in its scope when the measures adopted are reasonably related to the objectives of the search and not excessively intrusive in light of the age and sex of the student and the nature of the infraction." . . .

Perhaps the best that can be said generally about the required knowledge component of probable cause for a law enforcement officer's evidence search is that it raises a "fair probability," or a "substantial chance," of discovering evidence of criminal activity. The lesser standard for school searches could as readily be described as a moderate chance of finding evidence of wrongdoing.

The Events Leading Up to the Search

In this case, the school's policies strictly prohibit the nonmedical use, possession, or sale of any drug on school grounds, including "'[a]ny prescription or over-the-counter drug, except those for which permission to use in school has been granted pursuant to Board policy.'" A week before Savana was searched, another student, Jordan Romero (no relation of the school's administrative assistant), told the principal and Assistant Principal Wilson that "certain students were bringing drugs and weapons on campus," and that he had been sick after taking some pills that "he got from a classmate." On the morning of October 8, the same boy handed Wilson a white pill that he said Marissa Glines had given him. He told Wilson that students were planning to take the pills at lunch.

Wilson learned from Peggy Schwallier, the school nurse, that the pill was Ibuprofen 400 mg, available only by prescription. Wilson then called Marissa out of class. Outside the classroom, Marissa's teacher handed Wilson the day planner, found within Marissa's reach, containing various contraband items. Wilson escorted Marissa back to his office.

In the presence of Helen Romero, Wilson requested Marissa to turn out her pockets and open her wallet. Marissa produced a blue pill, several white ones, and a razor blade. Wilson asked where the blue pill came from, and Marissa answered, "'I guess it slipped in when *she* gave me the IBU 400s.'" When Wilson asked whom she meant, Marissa replied, "'Savana Redding.'" Wilson then enquired about the day planner and its contents; Marissa denied knowing anything about them. Wilson did not ask Marissa any followup questions to determine whether there was any likelihood that Savana presently had pills: neither asking when Marissa received the pills from Savana nor where Savana might be hiding them.

Schwallier did not immediately recognize the blue pill, but information provided through a poison control hotline indicated that the pill was a 200-mg dose of an anti-inflammatory drug, generically called naproxen, available over the counter. At Wilson's direction, Marissa was then subjected to a search of her bra and underpants by Romero and Schwallier, as Savana was later on. The search revealed no additional pills.

It was at this juncture that Wilson called Savana into his office and showed her the day planner. Their conversation established that Savana and Marissa were on friendly terms: while she denied knowledge of the contraband, Savana admitted that the day planner was hers and that she had lent it to Marissa. Wilson had other reports of their friendship from staff members, who had identified Savana and Marissa as part of an unusually

PRESCRIPTION DRUG ABUSE AMONG HIGH SCHOOL STUDENTS

Ever took prescription drugs without a doctor's prescription

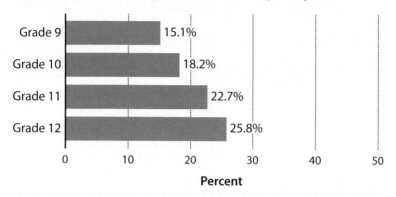

Taken from: Centers for Disease Control and Prevention, "Youth Risk Behavior Surveillance—United States, 2009," *Morbidity and Mortality Weekly Report (MMWR)*, June 4, 2010.

rowdy group at the school's opening dance in August, during which alcohol and cigarettes were found in the girls' bathroom. Wilson had reason to connect the girls with this contraband, for Wilson knew that Jordan Romero had told the principal that before the dance, he had been at a party at Savana's house where alcohol was served. Marissa's statement that the pills came from Savana was thus sufficiently plausible to warrant suspicion that Savana was involved in pill distribution.

This suspicion of Wilson's was enough to justify a search of Savana's backpack and outer clothing. If a student is reasonably suspected of giving out contraband pills, she is reasonably suspected of carrying them on her person and in the carryall that has become an item of student uniform in most places today. If Wilson's reasonable suspicion of pill distribution were not understood to support searches of outer clothes and backpack, it would not justify any search worth making. And the look into Savana's bag, in her presence and in the relative privacy of Wilson's office, was not excessively intrusive, any more than Romero's subsequent search of her outer clothing.

The Constitutionality of a Strip Search

Here it is that the parties part company, with Savana's claim that extending the search at Wilson's behest to the point of making her pull out her underwear was constitutionally unreasonable. The exact label for this final step in the intrusion is not important, though strip search is a fair way to speak of it. Romero and Schwallier directed Savana to remove her clothes down to her underwear, and then "pull out" her bra and the elastic band on her underpants. Although Romero and Schwallier stated that they did not see anything when Savana followed their instructions, we would not define strip search and its Fourth Amendment consequences in a way that would guarantee litigation about who was looking and how much was seen. The very fact of Savana's pulling her underwear away from her body in the presence of the two officials who were able to see her necessarily exposed her breasts and pelvic area to some degree, and both subjective and reasonable societal expectations of personal privacy support the treatment of such a search as categorically distinct, requiring distinct elements of justification on the part of school authorities for going beyond a search of outer clothing and belongings.

Savana's subjective expectation of privacy against such a search is inherent in her account of it as embarrassing, frightening, and humiliating. The reasonableness of her expectation (required by the Fourth Amendment standard) is indicated by the consistent experiences of other young people similarly searched, whose adolescent vulnerability intensifies the patent intrusiveness of the exposure. The common reaction of these adolescents simply registers the obviously different meaning of a search exposing the body from the experience of nakedness or near undress in other school circumstances. Changing for gym is getting ready for play; exposing for a search is responding to an accusation reserved for suspected wrongdoers and fairly understood as so degrading that a number of communities have decided that strip searches in schools are never reasonable and have banned them no matter what the facts may be.

The indignity of the search does not, of course, outlaw it, but it does implicate the rule of reasonableness as stated in *T.L.O.*, that "the search as actually conducted [be] reasonably related in scope to the circumstances which justified the interference in the first place." The scope will be permissible, that is, when it is "not excessively intrusive in light of the age and sex of the student and the nature of the infraction."

An Unreasonable Search

Here, the content of the suspicion failed to match the degree of intrusion. Wilson knew beforehand that the pills were prescription-strength ibuprofen and over-the-counter naproxen, common pain relievers equivalent to two Advil, or one Aleve. He must have been aware of the nature and limited threat of the specific drugs he was searching for, and while just about anything can be taken in quantities that will do real harm, Wilson had no reason to suspect that large amounts of the drugs were being passed around, or that individual students were receiving great numbers of pills.

Nor could Wilson have suspected that Savana was hiding common painkillers in her underwear. Petitioners suggest, as a truth universally acknowledged, that "students . . . hid[e] contraband in or under their clothing," and cite a smattering of cases of students with contraband in their underwear. But when the categorically extreme intrusiveness of a search down to the body of an adolescent requires some justification in suspected facts, general background possibilities fall short; a reasonable search that extensive calls for suspicion that it will pay off. But nondangerous school contraband does not raise the specter of stashes in intimate places, and there is no evidence in the record of any general practice among Safford Middle School students of hiding that sort of thing in underwear; neither Jordan nor Marissa suggested to Wilson that Savana was doing that, and the preceding search of Marissa that Wilson ordered yielded nothing. Wilson never even determined when Marissa had received the pills from Savana; if it had been a few days before, that would weigh heavily against any reasonable conclusion that Savana presently had the pills on her person, much less in her underwear.

In sum, what was missing from the suspected facts that pointed to Savana was any indication of danger to the students from the power of the drugs or their quantity, and any reason to suppose that Savana was carrying pills in her underwear. We think that the combination of these deficiencies was fatal to finding the search reasonable.

In so holding, we mean to cast no ill reflection on the assistant principal, for the record raises no doubt that his motive throughout was to eliminate drugs from his school and protect students from what Jordan Romero had gone through. Parents are known to overreact to protect their children from danger, and a school official with responsibility for safety may tend to do the same. The difference is that the Fourth Amendment places limits on the official, even with the high degree of deference that courts must pay to the educator's professional judgment.

We do mean, though, to make it clear that the *T.L.O.* concern to limit a school search to reasonable scope requires the support of reasonable suspicion of danger or of resort to underwear for hiding evidence of wrongdoing before a search can reasonably make the quantum leap from outer clothes and backpacks to exposure of intimate parts. The meaning of such a search, and the degradation its subject may reasonably feel, place a search that intrusive in a category of its own demanding its own specific suspicions.

> "The strip search was the most
> humiliating experience I have
> ever had."

The Student Plaintiff in *Redding* Describes Her Search by School Officials

Personal Narrative

Savana Redding

In the following viewpoint, a student recounts her experience being searched by school officials. The search was the result of a school official finding prescription pills on another student who claimed that she was the source of the pills. The author says she was questioned by the school official and denied ever bringing any pills to school. She details the search of her backpack and, when nothing was found, how she was ordered to strip to her underclothes, an experience that she believes violated her privacy. Savana Redding took her case all the way to the US Supreme Court in Safford Unified School District #1 v. Redding *(2009), wherein the court ruled that the strip search violated her constitutional rights.*

Savana Redding, "Affidavit of Savana Redding," pp. 1–4, *Redding v. Safford Unified School District #1*, United States District Court of Arizona, November 3, 2004.

I attended Safford Middle School ("Safford") for a portion of sixth grade, all of seventh grade and a portion of eighth grade. I was an honor roll student.

I am not aware of a history of drug abuse at the school nor do I believe that the school has a reputation of problems with substance abuse.

Before this incident, I had never been disciplined while I attended Safford.

The Day of the Interrogation

On October 8, 2003 while I was in Math class, vice-principal Kerry Wilson came into class and told me to collect my books and backpack and follow him to his office.

Once in his office, Mr. Wilson started discussing the importance of telling the truth. I told him I would tell the truth.

While Mr. Wilson was speaking, I noticed my planner on Mr. Wilson's desk. It was open and contained objects that were not mine. It contained several knives, a lighter and a cigarette, none of which were mine.

I recognized some of the items as belonging to Marissa Glines, another student at Safford.

At Marissa's request I had lent her my planner a couple of days before this incident. She said she had some things she wanted to hide from her parents, specifically cigarettes, a lighter and some jewelry.

When asked about the planner I admitted that it was mine, but indicated that none of the objects were mine and told Mr. Wilson that I had lent my planner several days earlier to Marissa.

Mr. Wilson then pointed to some pills on his desk. There were four white pills and a blue pill. He asked if I had seen these pills before. I said no.

Then Mr. Wilson told me that he had found the pills in Marissa's things and that someone had said that I was passing out prescription pills at school.

Savana Redding, center, was strip-searched by school officials looking for prescription-strength ibuprofen pills when she was thirteen years old. She and her lawyer, Adam Wolf, stand outside the US Supreme Court building in April 2009, after the court heard their case. © Roger L. Wollenberg/UPI/Landov.

I told Mr. Wilson that I had never brought any prescription pills to school and that I had never given any pills to any student at Safford.

Mr. Wilson then asked me if I would mind if they searched my stuff.

I knew that they would not find anything, so I agreed to the search. Mr. Wilson then called Mrs. Romero into the office.

They searched my backpack and found nothing. Then Mr. Wilson told Mrs. Romero to take me to the nurse's office.

The Humiliation of a Strip Search

That day I was wearing stretch pants without pockets and a T-shirt without pockets.

I went to the nurse's office. Mrs. Romero asked me to remove my jacket, socks and shoes. The school nurse, Mrs. Schwallier was in the bathroom washing her hands. When Mrs. Schwallier came out they told me to remove my pants and shirt.

I took off my clothes while they both watched. Mrs. Romero searched the pants and shirt and found nothing.

Then they asked me to pull my bra out and to the side and shake it, exposing my breasts. Then they asked me to pull out my underwear and shake it. They also told me to pull the underwear out at the crotch and shake it, exposing my pelvic area.

I was embarrassed and scared, but felt I would be in more trouble if I did not do what they asked. I held my head down so that they could not see that I was about to cry.

Then Mrs. Schwallier told me to put my clothes back on and to accompany Mrs. Romero back to the vice-principal's office.

Once back at Mr. Wilson's office, after he was advised that nothing was found in my clothes or my person, I was asked to sit in a chair outside of Mr. Wilson's office for approximately 2 1/2 hours.

While I sat in the chair, several individuals came and went from Mr. Wilson's office, including other students Jordan Romero and Chris Clark, a policeman, the principal Mr. Beeman and Marissa's dad, Mr. Glines.

At one point Mr. Beeman came out and told me he had heard that I stashed Marissa's stuff in my backpack.

After the incident, Chris Clark told me that when they searched him, they only asked him to empty his pockets, shake out his shirt and shake his pants up and down. He was not asked to remove any of his clothing.

I was finally allowed to return to class at approximately 12:00 P.M.

The strip search was the most humiliating experience I have ever had. Mrs. Romero and Mrs. Schwallier did not look away while I was taking off my clothes. They did nothing to respect my privacy.

They could have allowed me to remove my clothes in the bathroom stall, or behind a wall, or at least they could have turned their backs to me, but they did not.

I felt offended by the accusations made against me and violated by the strip search.

I was not given the opportunity to call my mother or other relative. After school that day my mother learned what happened. She was very upset and called to make an appointment with the Mr. Beeman.

My mother and I met with Mr. Beeman in his office. Mr. Beeman indicated that he did not think the strip search was a big deal because they did not find anything.

> *"There's still a difference between the rights we afford students and the rights we afford prison inmates. Just not a very big one."*

The Supreme Court Has Determined That Students Have Few Rights

Steve Chapman

In the following viewpoint, a columnist argues that students have very little freedom and a severely restricted right to privacy. The author approves of the US Supreme Court's conclusion in Safford Unified School District #1 v. Redding *(2009), but laments the extent to which the court has approved of ever-widening searches of students. He claims that with regard to the Fourth Amendment, students are treated in a manner dangerously similar to that of prison inmates. Steve Chapman is an editorial writer for the* Chicago Tribune.

Public schools are filled with eager, fresh-faced youngsters, and prisons contain many rough-looking adults with uninviting personalities. But put aside that difference and you find some important similarities between the two places—

government-run facilities where individuals are held for a specific number of years without their consent, at the mercy of their custodians.

A Small Victory for Student Privacy

For years, the Supreme Court has been doing its best to further blur the distinction by giving public-school officials the same powers as the warden of San Quentin. So it was a mild surprise last week [June 25, 2009] to learn there are some abridgments of freedom and invasions of privacy inflicted on children that the justices will not tolerate.

That's the good news for youngsters. The bad news is unless an administrator makes you take off your clothes, you're probably out of luck.

One day in the fall of 2003, a middle-school student in Safford, Ariz., was caught with contraband ibuprofen, which she said she had gotten from Savana Redding. The 13-year-old Savana was called to the office, where she denied knowing anything about the pills and agreed to a search of her belongings.

When it turned up nothing, an administrative assistant took her to the nurse's office and told her to remove her jacket, socks, and shoes. Still no pills.

That would have been the perfect moment for a sudden burst of common sense, inducing the school officials to admit defeat and let the girl get back to algebra. But the needed epiphany did not come to the adults. They ordered Savana to take off her shirt and pants—a step that also proved unavailing.

Were they done? No, they were not. In their relentless quest for illicit Advil, the officials refused to let considerations of modesty be an impediment. They insisted that Savana pull her bra and underpants away from her body to prove she was not hiding pills there. Again, they got nothing.

Last week, though, they got a rebuke from the Supreme Court. It has given principals and teachers great latitude in imposing control on children. But even justices who were indulgent

The decisions of the US Supreme Court have given schools authority to search a student's locker, purse, or backpack with little probable cause. © Steve Wisbauer/Stockbyte/Getty Images.

with past government intrusions gagged at the image of officials peeking into an adolescent's most private areas.

The Privacy Rights of Students

Justices Samuel Alito and Ruth Bader Ginsburg don't agree on many things. But they and six other justices (Clarence Thomas being the exception) joined in a decision that rejected abusing public-school students in the name of protecting them.

The Fourth Amendment, they noticed, says individuals shall not be subject to "unreasonable searches and seizures," and this search was flagrantly unreasonable. The mere possibility of finding pills in underpants is not enough, wrote Justice David Souter, to "make the quantum leap from outer clothes and backpacks to exposure of intimate parts."

School administrators might be forgiven for not knowing that. After all, the Supreme Court had previously allowed them to force students to undergo drug testing as a condition of participating in any extracurricular activity. Making students who have done nothing wrong produce a urine sample under the monitoring of a teacher, it insisted, was "not significant" as a breach of privacy.

The court had also permitted schools to search a kid's locker, backpack, and purse on even modest suspicion that some trivial school rule had been violated.

Justice John Paul Stevens complained that under these decisions, "a student detained by school officials for questioning, on reasonable suspicion that she has violated a school rule, is entitled to no more protection under the Fourth Amendment than a criminal suspect under custodial arrest." The Constitution's privacy protection, he said, has become "virtually meaningless in the school context."

Stevens did not exaggerate. Even in this case, the court was willing to tolerate making a 13-year-old girl strip to her underwear. It was the "exposure of intimate parts," not the exposure of everything else, that caused the justices to bridle. But if a more

AMERICAN TRUST IN THE COURTS

This graph shows the percentage of Americans who say they trust the US Supreme Court a great deal or a fair amount. It shows that trust and confidence in the judicial branch of the federal government, headed by the US Supreme Court, has fluctuated in recent decades.

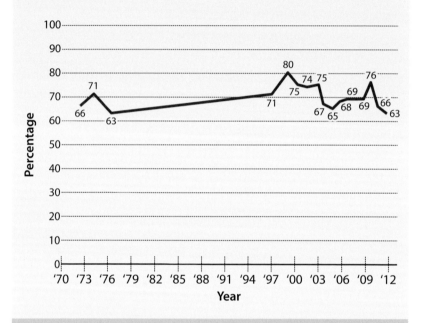

Taken from: Jeffrey M. Jones, "Supreme Court Approval Rating Dips to 46%," Gallup Politics, October 3, 2011. http://www.gallup.com/poll/149906/Supreme-Court-Approval-Rating -Dips.aspx

dangerous item had been sought or if there had been reason to think she was actually hiding a pill in her bra, the majority indicated, the search might have been perfectly acceptable.

So there's still a difference between the rights we afford students and the rights we afford prison inmates. Just not a very big one.

> *"Searches and seizures of students'*
> *cellular phones and laptops are*
> *permitted when there is a reasonable*
> *suspicion that the student is violating*
> *the law or the rules of the school."*

Seizures and Searches of Students' Phones and Laptops Are Constitutional

Kenneth T. Cuccinelli II

In the following viewpoint, the attorney general of Virginia con-
tends that searches of students' phones and laptops are constitu-
tional in certain situations; namely, when there is a reasonable
suspicion on the part of school officials that the student has broken
the law or violated school rules. The author argues that reasonable
suspicion of bullying is grounds for search and seizure, as is reason-
able suspicion of harboring sexually explicit material. Kenneth T.
Cuccinelli II became the attorney general for the state of Virginia
in 2010 and previously served as a state senator.

I am responding to your request for an official advisory opinion in accordance with § 2.2-505 of the *Code of Virginia*.

Searches of Student Phones and Laptops

You ask in what circumstances middle and high school principals and teachers may seize and search students' cellular phones and laptops to combat "cyber bullying" and how school officials can address student "sexting" without violating Virginia law themselves.

It is my opinion that searches and seizures of students' cellular phones and laptops are permitted when there is a reasonable suspicion that the student is violating the law or the rules of the school and, further, that school officials should not share explicit materials depicting minors with other school personnel, but rather that the material should be brought to the attention of the appropriate law enforcement agents.

The Fourth Amendment to the Constitution of the United States provides that "[t]he right of the people to be secure in their persons, house, papers, and effects, against unreasonable search and seizure, shall not be violated." This "prohibition on unreasonable searches and seizures applies to searches conducted by public school officials" [*New Jersey v. T.L.O.* (1985)]. "To be reasonable under the Fourth Amendment, a search ordinarily must be based on individualized suspicion of wrongdoing" [*Chandler v. Miller* (1997)]. The Supreme Court of the United States typically requires that a search be conducted only pursuant to a warrant supported by probable cause. When the purpose of a Fourth Amendment search is not to discover evidence of a crime, however, but is intended to serve some "special needs, beyond the normal need for law enforcement" [*T.L.O.*] the Supreme Court has held that a reasonable, articulable suspicion may be all that is necessary to satisfy constitutional requirements.

The supervision and operation of schools present "special needs" beyond normal law enforcement and, therefore, a different framework is justified. The United States Supreme Court concluded in *New Jersey v. T.L.O.* that "maintaining security and order in the schools requires a certain degree of flexibility in school disciplinary procedures . . . [that] preserves the informality of the

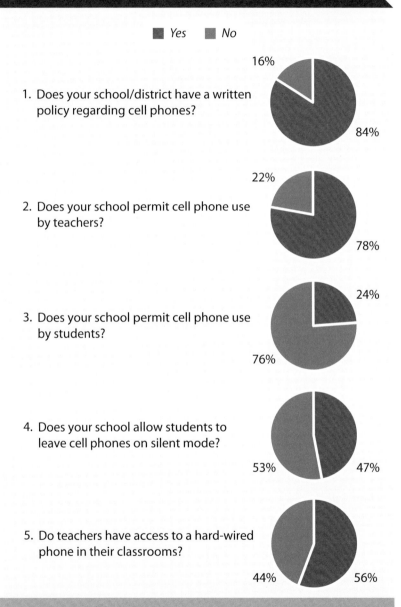

RESPONSES OF HIGH SCHOOL PRINCIPALS TO QUESTIONS ABOUT CELL PHONES AT SCHOOL, 2007

■ *Yes* ■ *No*

1. Does your school/district have a written policy regarding cell phones?

16%
84%

2. Does your school permit cell phone use by teachers?

22%
78%

3. Does your school permit cell phone use by students?

24%
76%

4. Does your school allow students to leave cell phones on silent mode?

53% 47%

5. Do teachers have access to a hard-wired phone in their classrooms?

44% 56%

Taken from: S. John Obringer and Kent Coffey, "Cell Phones in American High Schools: A National Survey," *The Journal of Technology Studies*, vol. 33, no. 1, Winter 2007.

student-teacher relationship." The Court recognized the competing interests that are distinct to the school environment: "On one side of the balance are arrayed the individual's legitimate expectation of privacy and personal security; on the other, the government's need for effective methods to deal with breaches of the public order." The court modified ordinary Fourth Amendment analysis in two significant ways. First, an "accommodation of the privacy interests of school children with the substantial need of teachers and administrators for freedom to maintain order in the schools does not require the strict adherence to the requirement that searches be based on probable cause." Second, the warrant requirement does not apply to school officials who search a student under their authority.

Accordingly, searches of a student's belongings—including an examination of the messages found on a cell phone or laptop—are justified if, when the search is made, the teacher or principal has "reasonable grounds for suspecting that the search will turn up evidence that the student has violated or is violating either the law or the rules of the school." In addition, the subsequent search must be "reasonably related to the objectives of the search and not excessively intrusive in light of the age and sex of the student and the nature of the infraction."

Advice for Specific Scenarios

Your first inquiry specifically presents the following scenario: a student reports to a teacher that he received a text message from another student that is either threatening or criminal or violates the school's bullying policy. You ask whether the teacher can seize the alleged bully's cellular phone and conduct a search of the outgoing text messages to investigate the claim. Recognizing that no court has considered the matter and that a definitive determination whether the situation you present creates a reasonable suspicion of wrongdoing depends on a complete and detailed set of facts, it is my general opinion that a search of a cellular phone by a school principal or teacher under these circumstances would be reasonable under the Fourth Amendment and the standard established in *New Jersey v. T.L.O.* Moreover, under *T.L.O.*, once a reasonable suspicion of wrongdoing exists, a search of a student's personal belongings does not require the student's consent or the consent of his parents.

Your second inquiry concerns whether a teacher who has discovered sexually explicit material on a student's cellular phone can show the material to another teacher or a principal for disciplinary purposes without violating Virginia law. The outcome of the inquiry depends on whether your question relates solely to sexually explicit material involving adults or whether the sexually explicit material involves children.

If a teacher, upon lawful search of a student's cellular phone, discovers sexually explicit material involving adults, he or she may show the material to a principal or another teacher for disciplinary purposes pursuant to any existing school policies without violating Virginia law. If, however, the discovered material involves a person under the age of eighteen, it may constitute child pornography, the knowing possession and distribution of which is prohibited under § 18.2-374.1:1. Any person who distributes such material shall be punished by five to twenty years imprisonment, and, therefore, prudence counsels that a teacher who discovers sexually explicit visual material involving a suspected minor during a legal search of a student's cellular phone should refrain from showing, transmitting, or distributing such material. Upon discovery of potential child pornography, the teacher or principal should promptly contact the appropriate law-enforcement agency within his jurisdiction and turn the material over to one of its authorized agents without distributing the material to others. The teacher discovering the material may, of course, discuss the nature of the material with a principal or another teacher for disciplinary purposes pursuant to the school's respective policies. As with the legal standard governing searches and seizures within the school context, a definitive determination of whether an action constitutes a criminal

According to the Virginia Attorney General, searches and seizures of students' cellular phones are permissible under the US Constitution if there is reasonable cause to believe the devices are being used for cyberbulling, "sexting," or otherwise violating school rules. © Roy Mehta/ Riser/Getty Images.

violation is a matter reserved to Commonwealth's Attorneys and the courts.

Accordingly, it is my opinion that searches of students' cellular phones and laptops by school officials are permitted when based on reasonable suspicion that the particular student is violating the law or the rules of the school and the search is "reasonably related to the objectives of the search and not excessively intrusive in light of the age and sex of the student and the nature of the infraction." In instances where a school official discovers sexually explicit material involving an identifiable minor, the official should refrain from showing, transmitting, or distributing that material to any other person except an authorized agent of the appropriate law-enforcement agency.

| "The Fourth Amendment is weaker than it was 50 years ago, and this should worry everyone."

Fourth Amendment Rights Have Become Weaker in Recent Years

David K. Shipler

In the following viewpoint, a writer argues that the Fourth Amendment guarantee of freedom from unreasonable searches and seizures has been eroding over the last several decades. He claims that the weakening of the right to privacy has been driven by the false belief that liberty and security are at odds with each other. The author warns that surrendering rights in the name of safety threatens the liberty of all. David K. Shipler is the author of The Rights of the People: How Our Search for Safety Invades Our Liberties *and creator of the blog* The Shipler Report.

This spring [2011] was a rough season for the Fourth Amendment. The [Barack] Obama administration petitioned the Supreme Court to allow GPS [global positioning system] tracking of vehicles without judicial permission. The Supreme Court ruled that the police could break into a house without a search warrant if, after knocking and announcing themselves, they heard what sounded like evidence being destroyed. Then it refused to see a Fourth Amendment violation where a citizen was jailed for 16 days on the false pretext that he was being held as a material witness to a crime.

The Erosion of the Fourth Amendment

In addition, Congress renewed Patriot Act provisions on enhanced surveillance powers until 2015, and the F.B.I. expanded agents' authority to comb databases, follow people and rummage through their trash even if they are not suspected of a crime.

None of these are landmark decisions. But together they further erode the privilege of privacy that was championed by Congress and the courts in the mid-to-late-20th century, when the Fourth Amendment's warrant requirement was applied to the states, unconstitutionally seized evidence was ruled inadmissible in state trials, and privacy laws were enacted following revelations in the 1970s of domestic spying on antiwar and civil rights groups.

For over a decade now, the government has tried to make us more secure by chipping away at the one provision of the Bill of Rights that pivots on the word "secure"—the Fourth Amendment's guarantee of "the right of the people to be secure in their persons, houses, papers and effects against unreasonable searches and seizures."

The Inseparability of Liberty and Security

The founding fathers, who sought security from government, would probably reject today's conventional wisdom that liberty and security are at odds, and that one must be sacrificed for the other. In their experience, the chief threat to individual security

Another Blow to the Fourth Amendment

The conservatives sitting on the Roberts Court [the US Supreme Court led by Chief Justice John Roberts] have cut deeply into our protection from unreasonable search and seizure guaranteed to Americans by the 4th Amendment to the Constitution. . . .

Jailers can now perform bodily strip searches on *anyone* brought in to a holding cell, no matter how minor the alleged infraction. . . .

I'm talking about individuals arrested for riding a bicycle without an audible bell, driving a car with a noisy muffler or failing to properly use a signal when making a left or right turn.

Rick Ungar, "Supreme Court Undercuts 4th Amendment Protections—Again," Forbes.com, April 2, 2012.

came from government itself, as in the house-to-house searches conducted by British customs officers under blanket "writs of assistance." After the Boston lawyer James Otis Jr. eloquently challenged the writs in 1761, John Adams, who was present in the crowded courtroom, wrote of the audience's rage, "Then and there the child independence was born."

Independent America's answer to those searches was the Fourth Amendment, with its requirement that law enforcement have probable cause to believe that evidence of a crime can be found at a particular place and time before a judge issues a warrant.

The ingenious feature of this demand is that it makes criminal investigations more efficient and accurate, even as it preserves liberty. If that rule and others in the Bill of Rights are followed,

US president George W. Bush signs the USA PATRIOT Act at the White House in 2006. Many argue that the act has greatly eroded the protection of citizens against unreasonable search and seizure under the Fourth Amendment. © AP Images/Ron Edmonds.

the police waste less time chasing false leads, make fewer erroneous arrests and leave the community safer.

In other words, the framers handed down a system in which liberty and security were fused, one inseparable from the other. So it is hard to see how safety has been enhanced by the post-9/11 expansion of counterterrorism surveillance, which has uncovered hardly any known plots and instead burdens analysts with so much irrelevant noise that they have trouble hearing the ominous melodies.

A recent study by the Breakthrough Institute found only two cases that benefited from the secret warrants made easier by the Patriot Act. The rest, the report concluded, "were broken open due to the combination of well-deployed undercover agents, information from citizen or undercover informants and tips from foreign intelligence agencies." The two exceptions were the Portland Seven, Oregon Muslims who tried to travel to Afghanistan to fight with the Taliban in 2001, and Najibullah Zazi, a Colorado resident from Afghanistan who pleaded guilty last year [2010] to planning a suicide attack in the New York City subways.

Two successes in nearly a decade might be enough to satisfy a fearful public, but it is worth noting that both cases began with old-fashioned tips—the first from a landlord, the second from Pakistani intelligence linking Mr. Zazi to Al Qaeda—and could have been pursued with the law enforcement tools available before 9/11.

The Danger of Surrendering Rights

The false dichotomy of liberty versus security is accompanied by another myth: that someone else's rights are always the ones at risk, that I can give up their rights for my safety. It seems a comfortable bargain. The terrorist is covertly monitored, the drug dealer is searched and the upstanding citizen is protected.

But it does not always work that way. The constitutional system of case law and precedent applies rulings on rights universally. So, legally, if a black man in a poor neighborhood can be stopped and frisked with minimal reason, so can a white woman in a rich neighborhood—even if the police tactics differ.

American history is replete with assaults on liberties that first target foreigners, minorities and those on the political margins, then spread toward the mainstream. The 1917 Espionage Act, for example, was used to prosecute American labor leaders and other critics of the government, and the 1798 Alien Enemies Act was revived after Pearl Harbor to intern American citizens of Japanese ancestry. A similar process is taking place now, as the F.B.I. has begun using counterterrorism tools to search, infiltrate and investigate groups of American peace activists and labor leaders in the Midwest.

The Fourth Amendment is weaker than it was 50 years ago, and this should worry everyone. "Uncontrolled search and seizure is one of the first and most effective weapons in the arsenal of every arbitrary government," Justice Robert H. Jackson, the former chief United States prosecutor at the Nuremberg trials [a series of military tribunals held to prosecute prominent members of the Nazi party], wrote in 1949. "Among deprivations of rights, none is so effective in cowing a population, crushing the spirit of the individual and putting terror in every heart."

Organizations to Contact

The editors have compiled the following list of organizations concerned with the issues debated in this book. The descriptions are derived from materials provided by the organizations. All have publications or information available for interested readers. The list was compiled on the date of publication of the present volume; the information provided here may change. Be aware that many organizations take several weeks or longer to respond to inquiries, so allow as much time as possible.

American Bar Association (ABA)
740 15th Street NW
Washington, DC 20005
(202) 662-1000 • fax (202) 662-1501
e-mail: crimjustice@abanet.org
website: www.abanet.org

The American Bar Association is a voluntary membership organization for professionals within the legal field that provides law school accreditation and works to promote justice, excellence of those within the legal profession, and respect for the law. The Section of Individual Rights and Responsibilities of the ABA is dedicated to addressing civil rights and civil liberties issues and ensuring that protection of individual rights remains a focus of legal and policy decisions. This section of the ABA publishes *Human Rights*, a quarterly magazine, and also makes available its *amicus curiae* briefs on behalf of parties before the courts in cases involving individual liberties.

American Center for Law and Justice (ACLJ)
PO Box 90555
Washington, DC 20090
(800) 296-4529
website: www.aclj.org

The American Center for Law and Justice is dedicated to protecting religious and constitutional freedoms. ACLJ has participated in numerous cases before the Supreme Court, Federal Court of Appeals, federal district courts, and various state courts regarding freedom of religion and freedom of speech. ACLJ has numerous memos and position papers available on its website, including "Protecting the Rights of Students."

American Civil Liberties Union (ACLU)

125 Broad Street, 18th Floor
New York, NY 10004
(212) 549-2500
e-mail: infoaclu@aclu.org
website: www.aclu.org

The American Civil Liberties Union is a national organization that works to defend civil rights as guaranteed in the US Constitution. It works in courts, legislatures, and communities to defend First Amendment rights, the right to equal protection, the right to due process, and the right to privacy. The ACLU publishes the semiannual newsletter *Civil Liberties Alert*, as well as briefing papers including "The Crisis in Fourth Amendment Jurisprudence."

Center for Public Education

1680 Duke Street
Alexandria, VA 22314
(703) 838-6722 • fax (703) 548-5613
e-mail: centerforpubliced@nsba.org
website: www.centerforpubliceducation.org

The Center for Public Education is a resource center set up by the National School Boards Association (NSBA). The Center for Public Education works to provide information about public education, leading to more understanding about our schools, more community-wide involvement, and better decision-making by school leaders on behalf of all students in their classrooms.

Among the many publications available on the center's website is "Search and Seizure, Due Process, and Public Schools."

Electronic Frontier Foundation (EFF)
54 Shotwell Street
San Francisco, CA 94110
(415) 436-9333 • fax (415) 436-9993
e-mail: information@eff.org
website: www.eff.org

Electronic Frontier Foundation works to promote the public interest in critical battles affecting digital rights and defends free speech, privacy, innovation, and consumer rights. It provides legal assistance in cases where it believes it can help shape the law. EFF publishes a newsletter and reports, and makes available its *amicus curiae* briefs on behalf of parties before the courts in cases involving electronic searches and seizures.

National Education Association (NEA)
1201 16th Street, NW
Washington, DC 20036
(202) 833-4000 • fax (202) 822-7974
website: www.nea.org

The National Education Association is an educator membership organization that works to advance the rights of educators and children. It focuses its energy on improving the quality of teaching, increasing student achievement, and making schools safe places to learn. Among the magazines that the NEA publishes are *NEA Today* and *Thought and Action*.

National Institute of Justice (NIJ)
810 Seventh Street, NW
Washington, DC 20531
(202) 307-2942
website: www.nij.gov

The National Institute of Justice, a component of the US Department of Justice, is dedicated to improving knowledge of crime and justice issues through science. NIJ provides information and tools to reduce crime and promote justice, particularly at the state and local levels. NIJ publishes the monthly *NIJ Journal*, available at its website, which includes such recent articles as "Debating DNA Collection."

National Youth Rights Association (NYRA)

1101 15th Street NW, Suite 200
Washington, DC 20005
(202) 835-1739
website: www.youthrights.org

The National Youth Rights Association is a youth-led national non-profit organization dedicated to fighting for the civil rights and liberties of young people. NYRA has more than seven thousand members representing all fifty states. It seeks to lower the voting age, lower the drinking age, repeal curfew laws, and protect student rights.

Office of Juvenile Justice and Delinquency Prevention (OJJDP)

810 Seventh Street, NW
Washington, DC 20531
(202) 307-5911
website: www.ojjdp.gov

The Office of Juvenile Justice and Delinquency Prevention, a component of the US Department of Justice, collaborates with professionals from diverse disciplines to improve juvenile justice policies and practices. OJJDP accomplishes its mission by supporting states, local communities, and tribal jurisdictions in their efforts to develop and implement effective programs for juveniles. Through its Juvenile Justice Clearinghouse, OJJDP provides access to fact sheets, summaries, reports, and articles from its journal, *Juvenile Justice*.

Student Drug-Testing Institute (SDTI)

8757 Georgia Avenue, Suite 1440
Silver Spring, MD 20910
(866) 956-SDTI (7384)
e-mail: SDTI@seiservices.com
website: sdti.ed.gov

The US Department of Education's Student Drug-Testing Institute provides information on many aspects of student drug-testing programs. The institute supports school efforts to implement drug-testing programs by recommending the necessary components for developing, implementing, and sustaining a confidential and effective program to promote drug-free students. Among the resources available at its website are publications about drug-testing programs and links to studies about drug testing.

For Further Reading

Books

William P. Bloss, *Under a Watchful Eye: Privacy Rights and Criminal Justice.* Santa Barbara, CA: Praeger, 2009.

Brian Carson and Catherine Ramen, *Understanding Your Right to Freedom from Searches.* New York: Rosen, 2012.

Thomas K. Clancy, *The Fourth Amendment: Its History and Interpretation.* Durham, NC: Carolina Academic Press, 2008.

Rolando V. del Carmen and Craig Hemmens, eds., *Criminal Procedure and the Supreme Court: A Guide to the Major Decisions on Search and Seizure, Privacy, and Individual Rights.* Lanham, MD: Rowman and Littlefield, 2010.

Dean Galiano, *The Fourth Amendment: Unreasonable Search and Seizure.* New York: Rosen Central, 2011.

Doreen Gonzales, *A Look at the Fourth Amendment: Against Unreasonable Searches and Seizures.* Berkeley Heights, NJ: Enslow, 2008.

William W. Greenhalgh, *The Fourth Amendment Handbook.* Chicago: Criminal Justice Section, American Bar Association, 2010.

Jesse V. Kessler, *The Fourth Amendment: Select Issues and Cases.* Hauppauge, NY: Nova Science, 2010.

Cynthia Lee, ed., *The Fourth Amendment: Searches and Seizures: Its Constitutional History and Contemporary Debate.* Amherst, NY: Prometheus Books, 2011.

Charles J. Russo and Ralph D. Mawdsley, *Searches, Seizures, and Drug Testing Procedures: Balancing Rights and School Safety.* Danvers, MA: LRP, 2008.

Christopher Slobogin, *Privacy at Risk: The New Government Surveillance and the Fourth Amendment*. Chicago: University of Chicago Press, 2007.

Periodicals and Internet Sources

Randal R. Befer, "Expansion of Police Power in Public Schools and the Vanishing Rights of Students," *Social Justice*, Spring–Summer 2002.

Larry K. Brendtro and Gordon A. Martin Jr., "Respect Versus Surveillance: Drug Testing Our Students," *Reclaiming Children and Youth: The Journal of Strength-Based Interventions*, Summer 2006.

Jacqui Cheng, "Expelled Student Sues Over 'Unreasonable' Cell Phone Search," *Ars Technica*, September 2009.

Rebecca N. Cordero, "No Expectation of Privacy: Should School Officials Be Able to Search Students' Lockers Without Any Suspicion of Wrong Doing?," *University of Baltimore Law Review*, Spring 2002.

Current Events, "Dog Fight: Drug-Sniffing Dogs in Schools Smell Trouble," December 9, 2005.

Floralynn Einesman and Howard Taras, "Drug Testing of Students: A Legal and Public Health Perspective," *Journal of Contemporary Health Law and Policy*, Spring 2007.

Ryan Grim, "Blowing Smoke: Why Random Drug Testing Doesn't Reduce Student Drug Use," *Slate*, March 21, 2006. www.slate.com.

Kristin Henning, "The Fourth Amendment Rights of Children at Home: When Parental Authority Goes Too Far," *William and Mary Law Review*, October 2011.

Tom Jacobs, "10 Supreme Court Cases Every Teen Should Know," *New York Times*, September 15, 2008.

Jennifer Kern, "Random Student Drug Testing Is Not the Answer," *Huffington Post*, May 7, 2008. www.huffingtonpost.com.

Nicole Klaas, "Suspicion in the Classroom," *Metroland,* September 28, 2006.

Linda McKay-Panos, "Privacy in Schools: Dogs, Lockers, Bodies, and Backpacks," *LawNow*, March/April 2009.

New York Times, "Unreasonable Search," April 19, 2009.

Stefanie Olsen, "Technology and the Law," *New York Times Upfront*, September 6, 2010.

Thomas H. Sawyer, "School Drug Strip Searches Limited in Scope," *Journal of Physical Education, Recreation, and Dance*, February 2010.

Jacob Sullum, "Advil Strip Search: Fourth Amendment Victory," *Reason*, November 2008.

Mark Walsh, "Testing the Limits of School Drug Tests," *Education Week*, March 13, 2002.

Washington Post, "Strip Searches in School," April 20, 2009.

Index

Von Raab, National Treasury Employees Union v. (1989), 49–50, 58–59

W

Wahkiakum School District, York v. (2008), 29

Warrants
  bypassing limitations, 114
  exceptions, 15
  exclusionary rule and, 20
  "fruit of the poisonous tree" and, 23
  judicial officials and, 16
  limitations of scope, 16–17, 22
  particularity requirement, 16–17
  preference of US Supreme Court, 15–17
  probable cause requirement, 16, 22, 45, 108
  thermal imaging and, 13–14, *15*
  vehicle tracking device and, 113–114

warrantless searches and seizures, 18–20, 83, 88–96
  See also School settings; Search and seizure

Washington (State) Supreme Court, 29

Weaver, Russell L., 10–20

West Virginia State Bd. of Ed. v. Barnette (1943), 32

White, Byron, 25, 30–39

Wilson, Kerry, 26, 88–96, 98–100

Winston Salem/Forsyth County School District (NC), 79–81

Wisconsin, Griffin v. (1987), 45, 47

Wright, Ingraham v. (1977), 33, 35

Writs of assistance, 11, 17, 115

Y

York v. Wahkiakum School District (2008), 29

Z

Zazi, Najibullah, 117